W9-DGE-329

C. P. CAVAFY

Poems

THE POEMS OF
C. P. CAVAFY

Translated into English
with a few notes

by

JOHN MAVROGORDATO

With an Introduction by

REX WARNER

1952
THE HOGARTH PRESS
LONDON

PUBLISHED BY
The Hogarth Press
LONDON
*
Clarke, Irwin & Co. Ltd.
TORONTO

FIRST PUBLISHED 1951
SECOND IMPRESSION 1952
PRINTED IN GREAT BRITAIN BY
BUTLER AND TANNER LTD
FROME AND LONDON

Contents

INTRODUCTION

Constantine Cavafy, who was born in 1863 and died in 1933, seems to have kept himself curiously aloof from the great revival of Greek poetry which was taking place during his life. During this period the Greeks of the mainland were becoming increasingly conscious of their newly won independence. Poets were transforming the language and, in the face of some conservative opposition, using the common speech in place of the artificial literary language known as *καθαρεύουσα*. Patriotism, sympathy with the literature of western Europe, a kind of triumphant lyricism mark the poetry of Palamas and of others who were accomplishing this splendid and powerful revival.

Cavafy, however, living in Alexandria, followed quite other methods. The main sources of his inspiration are the by-ways of ancient history and what to most people would appear as scandalous love affairs. Though profoundly conscious of the splendour and extent of the Greek tradition, his imagination finds its themes not in Homer nor in the age of Pericles, but in the Hellenistic blending of cultures and of races in cities like Alexandria or Antioch where Greek and Jew, pagan and Christian, sophist, priest and barbarian form a complicated and far from Periclean pattern. His world is the world which most English schoolmasters would describe as 'decadent'. It is a world without any of the obvious epic, lyric or tragic grandeurs. Yet it is a world that existed and exists. It can be examined minutely and dispassionately. And to this examination Cavafy brings a peculiar point of view together with a singular integrity.

His point of view is, in a way, the inversion of the heroic. He loves to insist not on some great completed accomplishment or successful quest, but on the importance of first steps or of incidents by the way. In the end the effect is often one of heroism, but it is of the quiet heroism of the individual rather than of the heroism of cause or state or professional strong man. In an early poem called "The First Step" he describes a young poet complaining to Theocritus that:

> It is two years now that I have been writing
> And I have finished only one idyl.

The young man goes on to suggest:

> from the first step here where I am now
> Unhappily I shall never go up.

Theocritus replies:

> These words of yours
> Are unbecoming words and blasphemous.
> Even if you are on the first step of all
> You should be happy and be proud of it.
> Here where you are is not a little way
> The so much you have done is a great glory.

Even to have taken the first step, he says, is to have given oneself a position different from and higher than the average. True that in "the city of ideas" you will find

> Lawgivers
> Who are not mocked by an adventurer.

But, difficult as further achievement is, there is no reason to be anything but thankful for what has been done already.

The tone of this early poem is very characteristic. On the one hand is the recognition of the extreme difficulty, even the improbability, of any great achievement: on the other hand is the insistence upon the unique value even of a conventionally minor experience, so long as it is accepted for what it is.

Much the same feeling is present in another early poem called "The God Abandons Antony". Here Cavafy is dealing with the story in Plutarch of how, before the fall of Alexandria and his own death, Antony heard the sound of music going away from the city. In Shakespeare's words:

> 'Tis the god Hercules, whom Antony loved,
> Now leaves him.

Cavafy, as again in his poem 'Ithaca', generalises the particular experience.

When suddenly there is heard at midnight
A company passing invisible
With wonderful music, with voices,—
Your fortune giving way now, your works
Which have failed, the plans of a lifetime
All turned illusions, do not mourn uselessly.

Instead the attitude to be adopted when losing Alexandria is one that "becomes one worthy as you were of such a city". It is to go firmly to the window and above all to refuse to believe that this experience is either meaningless or a dream. It is to:

Listen, your last enjoyment, to the sounds
The wonderful instruments of the mystic company,
And say farewell, farewell to Alexandria you are losing.

There is more here than stoicism, more than the dutiful acceptance of experience. There is the conscious, almost the sensual pride in saying 'yes' rather than saying 'no'. There is the curious paradox of defeat and failure being turned not into victory and success but into something almost or quite as respectable.

In 'Ithaca' also what is emphasised is the immense value of individual experience rather than the strained pursuit of an ideal or the heights and depths of cataclysmic events. Angry Poseidon, the savages and the Cyclops do not really exist or, if they do, they exist only in your own mind. Ithaca itself is only the excuse for a long journey. You must be in no hurry to arrive there. But of course it is immensely important. On your way to it you have visited the Phoenician trading stations, have acquired :

Mother of pearl and coral, amber and ebony,
And sensuous perfumes of every kind;
As much as you can get of sensuous perfumes.

And in the end, when you arrive at the poor and rocky island, you will have every reason to be satisfied.

Without Ithaca you would not have set out.
Ithaca has no more to give you now.

Poor though you find it, Ithaca has not cheated you,
Wise as you have become, with all your experience,
You will have understood the meaning of an Ithaca.

The early poems from which I have quoted are already well known. So too is another early poem, "Waiting for the Barbarians". Here is a fine ironical picture of Emperor, consuls and praetors, all in their best clothes, waiting to receive and to impress a barbarian army that never arrives. The people are excited and curious. Something strange and unexpected is on its way. But when, at nightfall, news comes that the barbarians have either disappeared or been annihilated, there is an increase of sudden gravity as the people return hurriedly to their houses.

> And now what will become of us without Barbarians?
> Those people were some sort of a solution.

Again it is a world that might be called 'decadent'—the world where a rich and civilised people await with keen curiosity the invasion of a barbarian army, not, it seems, concerned to repel the invaders by force, but interested in the situation, not unduly alarmed, and reasonably convinced that the foreigners will be impressed by red togas, bracelets, jewels and 'precious walking-sticks'. It is a scene very different from what could be imagined of Marathon or of Salamis, yet Cavafy's art is such that we are not out of sympathy with the crowd of sightseers either in their curiosity or in its disappointment. These studies of the unheroic have something of their own which, while it is not heroism, is a kind of dignity. It is the dignity and pathos of the real life which persists under whatever changes of government.

So, in the poem "Alexandrian Kings" which describes a magnificent military parade at which the children of Cleopatra are invested with the most high sounding titles, Cavafy re-creates an atmosphere which seems more real, more, in a sense, historical than that of Plutarch or of a professional historian. He makes no mention of Julius Caesar or of Antony. Cleopatra is only referred to incidentally. What he sees are the gay crowds coming to the spectacle, the royal children, particularly Caesarion:

> His shoes were tied with white ribbons
> Embroidered with rosy-coloured pearls.
> They called him rather more than the little ones,
> Him they called King of Kings.

There is no direct reference to the future fate of Caesarion or the collapse of Antony's and Cleopatra's ambitions. Instead, simply:

> The Alexandrians understood of course
> That this was only words and play acting.

And yet, with their understanding, knowing what it was all worth, they were enchanted by the spectacle.

The picture of a youth standing in a pink dress at a splendid parade moves Cavafy's imagination more than does the love of Antony and Cleopatra or the successes of Octavius. It is perhaps an unusual point of view, but it is a view of reality. In a later poem Cavafy returns to the theme of Caesarion. He finds the history of the Ptolemies boring:

> All famous, strong and full of noble deeds;
> Their every enterprise the top of wisdom.

And then, in his reading, occurs an unimportant mention of Caesarion. The poet immediately builds up in his imagination a figure of "dreamlike and attractive loveliness". He does not mention the fact that he is the child of Julius Caesar and of Cleopatra. He thinks of him after the fall of Alexandria:

> Pale and tired, idealistic in your grief,
> Still hoping that they would have mercy on you,
> The baser sort—chattering their "Too many Caesars".

There is another poem, written in 1926, and called "In a Township of Asia Minor", where the great names of Antony and Octavius are treated most characteristically. The battle of Actium has been commemorated in poetry of the very highest order. There is the Ode of Horace. There is Shakespeare, who makes Antony say:

> Hark! the land bids me tread no more upon 't;
> It is asham'd to bear me.

Cavafy is interested in a different kind of truth from that which inspires Horace or Shakespeare. He takes the point of view of a small town whose inhabitants have expected Antony to win and have composed already a flattering address to him. In fact it is a matter of complete indifference to these humble people which of the great emperors wins the decisive battle. They therefore make a simple alteration in their address.

> The news about the result of the sea-fight, at Actium,
> Were certainly unexpected.
> But there is no need for us to compose a new address.
> Let only the name be changed. Instead of (there
> In the last lines) "Having delivered the Romans
> From the disastrous Octavius,
> The burlesque Caesar,"
> Now we will put, "Having delivered the Romans
> From the disastrous Antony."
> The whole text fits in beautifully.

There is much more than cynicism in such a poem. It expresses an intelligible and a respectable truth, different indeed from the truth of Shakespeare, but still true.

Many poems of Cavafy could be cited as evidence for his invariable refusal to take up anything that could be called a conventional point of view. The epitaph of Aeschylus is criticised by the young men of Sidon, because it refers to Marathon rather than to the tragedies. The emperor Julian is attacked, not for paganism but for priggishness, for "His graceless prudery; his ridiculous beard". Words like 'politics', 'religion' and 'philosophy' are never abstractions, but are always seen in some real, and usually rather surprising, context. For example, in the poem, "From the school of the renowned philosopher", he writes:

> He remained a pupil of Ammonius Sakkas for two years;
> But philosophy bored him and so did Sakkas.

The young man whom he imagines then goes in for politics. But "the Governor was a fool" and the officials spoke very indifferent Greek. Religion rather attracted him. It would be amusing to offend his parents by becoming a Christian. But then they might cut off his allowance.

> All the same he had to do something. He became a client
> Of the corrupt houses of Alexandria.

He is fortunate in being good looking. His beauty should last for ten years. After the ten years have gone he may perhaps look up old Sakkas again, if he is not dead;

> Or finally, to politics too it was possible
> He might return—praiseworthily remembering
> His family traditions, his duty to his country,
> And other sounding matters of the sort.

What was it that gave Cavafy the power to produce poetry of such integrity, of such individual insight? He is aided certainly by his discovery of what amounts to a personal mythology. Imaginary or real characters from the Hellenistic court of Asia, Macedonia or Egypt somehow provide him (as has been well pointed out by Dr. C. M. Bowra)[1] with symbols that have the same appropriateness to his own genius as were to Yeats the mythologies of ancient Ireland or to T. S. Eliot, in "The Waste Land", the stories concerning the Holy Grail. So to Cavafy the secondary characters of ancient or Byzantine history—Galba, Caesarion, Orophernes—the imagined life of Antioch or Alexandria, where creeds and races were mixed, but where life was lived, provide the exactly appropriate symbols for the expression of a modern and unique outlook on the world. It is the outlook of a mind that is disillusioned, but never, in spite of appearances, cynical; of a meticulous critic, who loves the material exposed to the critical faculties. Yet it is poetry, not criticism, that we read and admire in Cavafy. Together with and underneath the controlled attitude, the steady point of view, we find the sudden flash of insight, the vigorous assertion of emotion. If we are to take the poet's own word for it, love affairs of a disreputable character were a source of immense inspiration.

> Under the dissolute living of my youth
> Were being formed the intentions of my poetry,
> The province of my art was being planned.

---

[1] "Constantine Cavafy and the Greek Past" in "The Creative Experiment"—an essay to which I have been deeply indebted in writing this introduction.

And there is another poem, entitled "Their Beginning", the first lines of which are:

> The consummation of their lawless pleasure
> Was done. They rose up from the mattress;
> And hurriedly they dress themselves without speaking,

There is, or appears to be, nothing lyrical about the experience, but the poem concludes with the lines:

> But for the artist how his life has gained.
> Tomorrow, the next day or years after will be written
> The lines of strength that here had their meaning.

Such poems as these are characteristic of Cavafy and reveal that the sources of his inspiration are not confined to his studies of ancient history. The fastidious moral and aesthetic sense of T. S. Eliot will reject or only use for purposes of denigration the "one-night cheap hotels". Cavafy is equally fastidious, but in a very different way. In such places he finds the life that exists even without Antony and Octavius, the valued experiences that give value to an Ithaca which otherwise is of little account. So, in a late poem, "The Mirror in the Hall", he describes an old mirror in a rich house. Into the hall, carrying a parcel for delivery, comes

> A very handsome boy, assistant at a tailor's
> (On Sundays an amateur athlete).

While waiting for the receipt this boy goes to the mirror to straighten his tie; the receipt is brought to him and he leaves the house.

> But the old mirror which had seen, and seen,
> In the many years it had been
> In existence, thousands of things and faces;
> The old mirror was glad now
> And was proud to have received upon itself
> That entire beauty for a few minutes.

Cavafy in general finds his "entire beauty" in what to many would seem to be unlikely places. What matters is that he found it, finding also at the same time a kind of truth, which has a peculiar relevance for the modern world. He is aware of all kinds of complexity, but not for that reason tempted into hysteria, exaggeration or over-emphasis. His quiet style and his choice of subject exactly represent his genius which accepts life without extravagant illusions. Yet in this particular act of acceptance he has somehow transformed what was there before. He has not only taken and described but created and discovered a world.

REX WARNER

1949

TRANSLATOR'S NOTE

This translation was originally made in 1937, at the request of some of Cavafy's English friends, from the complete edition published in Alexandria in 1935; but it remained unpublished. It has been revised and rewritten from beginning to end, I hope with considerable improvement, for the present publication.

I have always tried to keep my versions as literal as possible, translating line for line, and as far as possible word for word. I have sometimes been deflected from this ideal by the attempt to represent the rhymes and the rhyme-patterns of the original; but I don't think I have been deflected very far; and on the few occasions when I have had for the sake of an obstinate rhyme to put in anything which is not in the Greek, I have added a cautionary note. It should be remembered that the language of the original is seldom easily colloquial, and sometimes deliberately stiff and pedantic.

In the notes I have tried to give the smallest amount of historical information necessary for the understanding of the poems, and references only to the most obvious sources in ancient authors. Nearly all the references now given I had already noted in 1937; but since that date I have had the advantage of reading three books in Greek by the poet's friend, Mr. Timos Malános—*O Poiêtês K. P. Kabáfês* (Athens, 1933); *Peri Kabafê* (Athens, 1935); and *Mythologia tês Kabafikês Politeias* (Alexandria, 1943)—and in some cases, which I have tried always to acknowledge, I have taken from Mr. Malános some references which had previously escaped me. Anyone who wants to study the poet's work below the surface must begin by reading the investigations of Mr. Malános, even if he does not always like them. A recent study, more complete in some ways, is that by Mr. Michael Perides, *O Bios kai to Ergo tou Konstantinou Kabafê* (Athens, 1948). In English there are notable papers by Mr. E. M. Forster in *Pharos and Pharillon* (Hogarth Press, 1923); by Mr. R. Liddell in *Horizon* (September 1948); and by C. M. Bowra in *The Creative Experiment* (1949). The best edition of Cavafy's poems now obtainable is published in Athens (*Ikaros*, 1949). Mr. G. K. Katsimbalis published a Cavafy Bibliography in Athens in 1943, followed by a Supplement in 1944.

In the transliteration of proper names I prefer the system of transcribing Greek into English letter by letter, and have used it wherever possible, writing Demetrios rather than Demetrius, Kaisarion rather than Caesarion, Aristoboulos and Iannaios rather than Aristobulus and Jannaeus; but of course names like Caesar and Antony and Ptolemy are so familiar that they have to be accepted in their English forms; and I know that I have sometimes used both forms with deliberate inconsistency.

J. M.

Oxford 1945
London 1951

I

DESIRES

Like beautiful bodies dead that had not grown old
And they shut them up, with tears in a splendid tomb adorning
With roses at their heads and jasmine at their feet—
Desires are like that, desires that have grown cold
And not been satisfied; never vouchsafed one sweet
Night time of pleasure or one gleam of morning.

2

VOICES

Voices ideal and beloved
Of those who have died, or of those
Who are lost for us like the dead.

Sometimes in dreams they speak to us;
Sometimes within thinking the brain hears them.

And with the sound of them for a moment return
Sounds from the first poetry of our life—
Like music, at night, in the distance, that dies away.

3

PRAYER

The sea has taken a sailor to its deeps.—
Unknowing all the time his mother keeps

A candle burning at the Virgin's shrine,
That he may come again and skies be fine—

She listens all the time for the wind blowing.
But while she says her prayers, the Image, knowing,

Listens as in solemnity and pain,
Knowing her son will never come again.

This is an exercise in identical or homophonous rhymes—cf. no. 15—which cannot be reproduced in English.

4

THE FIRST STEP

There was complaining to Theocritus
One day the young poet Eumenes:
"It is two years now that I have been writing
And I have finished only one idyl.
It is my only work that is complete.
Alas, it's high I see,
And very high the stair of Poesy;
And from the first step here where I am now
Unhappily I shall never go up."
Then Theocritus said: "These words of yours
Are unbecoming words and blasphemous.
Even if you are on the first step of all
You should be happy and be proud of it.
Here where you are is not a little way;
The so much you have done is a great glory.
And even this the first and lowest step
Is much removed up from the common world.
In order to set foot upon this step
You have to be and have the right to be
A citizen of the city of ideas.
And in that city it is difficult
And it is rare that you should be enfranchised.
In that assembly you find Lawgivers
Who are not mocked by an adventurer.
Where you have come is not a little way;
This much that you have done is a great glory."

5

AN OLD MAN

An old man with a newspaper
Sits huddled at a table there
  Alone with all the noise around.
He thinks abject in age's fears
How little he enjoyed the years
  When he was strong and sane and sound.
He understands he's old; he knows.
And yet the time of youth still glows—
How short the road!—like yesterday.
He trusted Prudence—how absurd!—
She tricked him with a lying word:
  "Plenty of time. Another day."
Ardours restrained, the sacrifice
Of joy—to have been vainly wise
  Is mocked by every chance that's gone . . .
But with his thoughts and memories deep
Presently dazed, he falls asleep
  Over the table all alone.

6

CANDLES

The days of the future stand in front of us
Like a line of candles all alight—
    Golden and warm and lively little candles.
The days that are past are left behind,
A mournful row of candles that are out;
The nearer ones are still smoking,
    Candles cold, and melted, candles bent.
I don't want to see them; their shapes hurt me,
It hurts me to remember the light of them at first.
    I look before me at my lighted candles.
I don't want to turn round and see with horror
How quickly the dark line is lengthening,
How quickly the candles multiply that have been put
        out.

7
THERMOPYLAE

Honour to those whoever in their lives
Have set the bounds and guard Thermopylae.
Never moving from the line of duty;
Righteous and fair in all their actions,
With sympathy as well and with compassion;
If they are rich, generous, and if again
They are poor, generous in little things,
Still helping others as much as they can;
Always speaking the truth,
Yet without bitterness against the liars.

And again greater honour becomes them
When they foresee (and many do foresee)
That Ephialtes will be there in the end,
And that the Medes, at last, they will get through.

8

CHÈ FECE . . . IL GRAN RIFIUTO

To certain men when there comes a day
  They must say the great Yes or the great No.
  Whoever he is will straightway show,
Who has Yes within him ready to say;

And on he goes and honour ensues him.
  He never repents who has once denied;
  He would say No again, if he were tried.
Yet that proper No all his life subdues him.

9

THE SOULS OF THE OLD MEN

In their poor old bodies for their sins
The old men's souls remain,
Poor things how full of pain
And how sick they are of the wretched life they're trailing,
And how they love it and tremble to think of it failing,
Contradictory and muddled
Souls, tragicomically huddled
There in their poor old devastated skins.

10

INTERRUPTION

We interrupt the godly working power,
Senseless and hurried creatures of an hour.
In Phthian and in Eleusinian halls
Demeter now and Thetis still design
In flames and rolling smoke the work benign.
But always from the royal apartment calls
Metaneira, terrified and disarrayed,
And rushes in, or Peleus is afraid.

Metaneira was the queen of Eleusis who employed Demeter, on her wanderings, as a nurse, but interrupted when she saw the nurse putting the baby Demophoon in the fire to make him immortal. See *Homeric Hymn to Demeter*, 231 ff.

Peleus, King of Thessaly, married the Nereid Thetis, who wanting to know if their children had inherited her own immortality began throwing them into the fire; Peleus, however, interrupted her in time to save Achilles. This is the usual form of the story; but the present poem requires a variant according to which Thetis was only trying to burn away the mortal part of her children and so make them immortal.

II

THE WINDOWS

In these dark chambers here what weary days
I spend, walk up and down as in a maze
To find the windows.—Only to unclose
One of these windows will be some relief.—
But somehow windows this room hasn't got,
Or I can't find them. Perhaps I'd better not.
Perhaps the light would be another grief.
What fresh surprises there might be, who knows?

12

TROJANS

In our misfortunes our exertions are,
All our exertions, like those of the Trojans.
We do succeed a bit; and then a bit
We're ready to take on; and we begin
To have some confidence and some good hopes.

But something always turns up and stops us.
Achilles in the trench in front of us
Starts up and with loud shoutings frightens us.—

Our efforts are like those of the Trojans.
We think that with decision and daring
We shall change the animosity of fate,
And we go out and stand up to fight.

But when the great crisis comes,
Our daring and our decision are lost;
Our soul is agitated, and relaxes;
And all around about the walls we run
Seeking to get out of it by flight.

And yet our fall is certain. Up above,
Up on the walls the wailing has begun.
Memories weeping and sensations of the past.
Bitterly for us weep Priam and Hecuba.

13
THE FOOTSTEPS

On ebony bedstead, adorned
With coral eagles, soundly sleeps
Nero—unconscious, quiet, happy;
Blooming in the fleshly health
And lovely ardour of his youth.

But in the alabaster hall which closes
The ancient shrine of the Aenobarbi
How unquiet are his Lares. Tremble
All the little household gods and try
To hide their insignificant bodies.
Because they have heard a terrible sound,
A deadly sound ascending the staircase,
Iron footfalls that are shaking the stairs;
And fainting now the miserable Lares
Huddle in the recesses of the shrine,
One over another tumbling and stumbling,
One little god falls on top of another;
They understand the meaning of that sound,
And now they know the footfalls of the Avengers.

14

MONOTONY

Monotonous day another day succeeds
Monotonous, identical.   Once done
All will be done over again, the same deeds—
The similar minutes find us and are gone.

Month brings another month. So one may guess
Easily what is coming; and the sorrow
Of yesterday is but a weariness.
Tomorrow seems no longer like a morrow.

15

WALLS

Without consideration, without pity, without caring
They have built all around me these great high walls.

And now I can only sit in here despairing.
I can think of nothing else but my fate, and the thought of it
galls.

Because I had so many things to do outside.
When they were building the walls why didn't I take more care?

But I never noticed any noise of the builders. Undescried
They have shut me up away from the world out there.

This is, like no. 3, an exercise in homophonous rhymes which cannot be reproduced in translation.

16

WAITING FOR THE BARBARIANS

What are we waiting for all crowded in the forum?
The Barbarians are to arrive today.
Within the Senate-house why is there such inaction?
The Senators making no laws what are they sitting there for?
Because the Barbarians arrive today.
What laws now should the Senators be making?
When the Barbarians come they'll make the laws.

Why did our Emperor get up so early in the morning?
And at the greatest city gate why is he sitting there now,
Upon his throne, officially, why is he wearing his crown?
Because the Barbarians arrive today.
The Emperor is waiting to receive
Their Leader. And in fact he has prepared
To give him an address. On it he has
Written him down all sorts of names and titles.

Why have our two Consuls gone out, both of them, and the Praetors,
Today with their red togas on, with their embroidered togas?
Why are they wearing bracelets, and all those amethysts too,
And all those rings on their fingers with splendid flashing emeralds?
Why should they be carrying today their precious walkingsticks,
With silver knobs and golden tops so wonderfully carved?
Because the Barbarians will arrive today;
Things of this sort dazzle the Barbarians.

And why are the fine orators not come here as usual
To get their speeches off, to say what they have to say?
Because the Barbarians will be here today;
And they are bored with eloquence and speechmaking.

Why should this uneasiness begin all of a sudden,
And confusion. How serious people's faces have become.
Why are all the streets and squares emptying so quickly,
And everybody turning home again so full of thought?
 Because night has fallen and the Barbarians have not come.
 And some people have arrived from the frontier;
 They said there are no Barbarians any more.

 And now what will become of us without Barbarians?—
 Those people were some sort of a solution.

17

TREACHERY

"Then though there are many other things that we praise in Homer, this we will not praise . . . nor shall we approve of Aeschylus when his Thetis says that Apollo, singing at her wedding,

'Foretold the happy fortunes of her issue
Their days prolonged from pain and sickness free,
And rounding out the tale of heaven's blessings
Raised the proud paean making glad my heart.
And I believed that Phoebus' mouth divine
Filled with the breath of prophecy could not lie.
But he himself the singer . . .
Is now himself the slayer of my son.' "

Plato, *Republic*, 383 B (translation by Paul Shorey, Loeb Classics).

When they were marrying Thetis and Peleus
Apollo rose up at the splendid table
And called them blessed, the newly married pair,
For the issue that should spring from their union.
He said: Him shall no sickness ever touch
And he shall have a long life.—When he said this,
Thetis rejoiced greatly, because the words
Of Apollo himself who knew about prophesying
Seemed to her to be a surety for her child.
And when Achilles was growing up, and
His beauty was the praise of Thessaly,
Thetis used to remember the god's words.
But one day there came old men with tidings,
And told about the killing of Achilles at Troy.
And Thetis rent her purple clothes;
She began to take off and to fling away
On to the ground her bracelets and her rings.
And in her mourning she minded of old,
And she asked what he was doing, Apollo the wise,

Where went the poet who at the feast
Spoke so well, the prophet, what was he about,
When they were killing her son in his first youth.
Then the old men answered her that Apollo,
Himself in person had come down to Troy,
And with the Trojans he had killed Achilles.

The original is written in the metre of "The Queen was in the parlour eating bread and honey" (the Latin "Saturnian").

18

THE FUNERAL OF SARPEDON

Heavy sorrow has Zeus. Sarpedon has
Been killed by Patroklos; and now advance
The son of Menoitios and the Achaeans, his body
Hoping to seize and to dishonour it.

Zeus, however, does not like this at all.
His beloved child—that he left
To be destroyed: so it was ordained—
At least he will do honour to it dead.
He sends, look, Phoibos down into the plain
Instructed that the body must be looked after.

The hero's corpse with reverence and with grief
Phoibos lifts up and takes it to the river.
He washes away the dust and the blood;
Closes the dreadful wounds, not leaving
Any trace to show; of ambrosia
Pours over it the perfumes; and in splendid
Olympian raiment clothes.
The skin he whitens; and with a pearly
Comb the hair he combs out all black;
The lovely limbs arranges and lays them down.

Now like a young king he looks, a chariot driver—
In his twenty-fifth year or twenty-sixth—
Resting after he has won,
With a chariot all gold and very fast horses,
The prize in a famous competition.

So when Phoibos had completed
His charge, he called the two brothers,
Sleep and Death, commanding them
To take the body into Lykia, the rich land.

And towards that rich place, to Lykia
They journeyed, these two brothers
Sleep and Death, and when they had arrived
At the door of the royal house
They handed over the body covered with glory,
And turned to their other cares and services.

There when they received it, in the house, began
With processions, and honours, and lamentations,
And with abundant libations from sacred bowls,
And with all things becoming, the sad burial;
Afterwards skilled labourers from the city
And famous workers in stone
Came and made the tomb and the pillar.

Irregular iambics. Adapted from *Iliad*, XVI, 665–683.

19

BACCHUS AND HIS CREW

Damon (and of craftsmen he's
Best in all Peloponnese)
In Parian marble carves the crew
Of Bacchus. First with glory due
The god, with power in his stride.
Licence next; and at his side
Drunkenness pours the Satyrs wine
From a jar that ivies twine.
Near them languid Winesweet lies
Bringing sleep, with half-closed eyes.
Two singers, Tune and Sweetsong, stand
Below, while Revelry at hand
Never lets plenty's lamp go out;
And strict Ceremony devout.—
These Damon makes; and making these
Once and again thinks on the fees
From Syracuse's king to come,
Three talents, quite a proper sum.
Add this to what he's got, he can
Live like a rich and serious man,
In politics—what joy to grace
The Council, and the market-place!

20

THE HORSES OF ACHILLES

But when they saw that Patroklos was dead,
Who was so young, and strong, and brave of heart,
The horses of Achilles so did start
To weep; and their immortal part rebelled
Against the work of death they there beheld;
Shaking their heads, waving their manes unshorn,
And tramping on the ground, as if to mourn
For Patroklos, knowing his soul was fled
Away from empty flesh,—his spirit shed,—
Without breath,—weaponless,—
Returned from life to the great Nothingness.

The tears of the immortal horses there
Zeus saw and grieved. "At Peleus' wedding-day"
He said "unwise and thoughtless was my way;
Better my horses never to bestow
Unfortunate! What would you down below
With wretched man who is the toy of fate,
Horses whom death and age no wise await?
The woes of time torment you, and men snare
In their own miseries." Yet for the care
Of death perpetual
The noble horses let the tears downfall.

Adapted from *Iliad*, XVII, 426–447.

21

THERE HE IS!

A stranger in Antioch—from Edessa—he must keep
Writing and writing—unknown. But, there, the last lay
Is done in the end. And that makes eighty-three

Poems in all. But the poet is weary
Of so much writing, and all that scanning,
And the strain of all that Greek phrase planning,
And everything about it now seems dreary.—

But all of a sudden out of despondency
Lifts him the wonderful thought of hearing them say
That is the man! as Lucian dreaming heard in his sleep.

See Lucian, *The Dream*, § 11 (Lucian, Loeb Classics, vol. 3, p. 224).

22

KING DEMETRIOS

> "So he went into his tent, and cast a blacke cloake about his face, in stead of his rich and stately cloake he was wont to wear, not like unto a King, but like a common player . . .; and then secretly stole away."
>
> Plutarch, *Life of Demetrios*
> (North's translation)

When the Macedonians abandoned him,
And plainly showed that they preferred Pyrros,
The King Demetrios (for he was noble
In spirit), not at all—so they said—
Bore himself like a king. He went away
And took off his golden robes,
And threw away the shoes from off his feet
The shoes all purple-dyed. In simple clothes
He dressed himself quickly and fled away—
Doing just like any play actor,
Who, when the play comes to an end,
Changes his wear and goes away.

Besides the passage from Plutarch quoted in the heading, see also Lucian's dialogue, *The Cock*, § 26 (Lucian, Loeb Classics, vol. 2, p. 227.)

23

THE TOWN

You said "I'll go to another land, to other seaways wandering,
Some other town may yet be found better than this,
Where every effort of mine is a writ of guiltiness;
And my heart seems buried like a corpse. My mind—
How long is it to be in this decay confined?
Wherever I turn, whenever I lift my eyes,
The blackening ruins of my life arise,
Where I have spent so many years spoiling and squandering."

"You'll find no other places, no new seas in all your wanderings,
The town will follow you about. You'll range
In the same streets. In the same suburbs change
From youth to age; in this same house grow white.
No hope of another town; this is where you'll always alight.
There is no road to another, there is no ship
To take you there. As here in this small strip
You spoiled your life, the whole earth felt your squanderings."

A translation of the second stanza by G. Valassopoulo will be found in E. M. Forster's *Pharos and Pharillon*, p. 77.

24

SATRAPY

What a misfortune for you who are made
For beautiful and great accomplishments
This unfair destiny of yours should always
Deny you still encouragement and success;
That vulgar habits should ever hinder you,
Meanness prevent you, and indifferences.
And how dreadful the day when you surrender
(The day you let yourself go and you surrender),
And you go off wayfaring to Susa,
You go to the Great King Artaxerxes,
Who very kindly puts you in his court,
Offers you satrapies and all the rest of it.
And you accept them with despair,
The very things which you don't want at all.
Your soul seeks other things, and cries for them;
The praises of the crowd and of the Sophists,
The difficult and inestimable applause,
The Assembly, and the Theatre, and the Crowns.
How will you get all this from Artaxerxes?
How will you find these in your satrapy?
What will your life be like without all these?

25

THE IDES OF MARCH

Be afraid of grandeurs, O my soul;
And if you cannot conquer your ambitions
With hesitation always and precautions
Follow them up. And as you go ahead
So be attentive and meticulous.

And when you arrive at your glory, now you are Caesar,
When you put on the figure of such fame,
Then take particular care when you go out into the street,
One in authority conspicuous with your escort,
If it happen then that out of the crowd should press
Near you some Artemidoros with a letter,
And say hurriedly, "Read this immediately—
They be matters of great weight and touch you nearly,"
Do not fail to stop. Do not fail to put off
Every interview or business. Do not fail those various
People who greet and salute you to put them aside
(You can see them later). Let it wait even
The Senate itself; and at once you must read
The grave writings of Artemidoros.

See Plutarch's *Life of Julius Caesar* (and Shakespeare's *Julius Caesar*, iii. 1).

26

THE GOD ABANDONS ANTONY

When suddenly there is heard at midnight
A company passing invisible
With wonderful music, with voices,—
Your fortune giving way now, your works
Which have failed, the plans of a lifetime
All turned illusions, do not mourn uselessly.
As one prepared long since, courageously,
Say farewell to her, to Alexandria who is leaving.
Above all do not be tricked, never say it was
All a dream, and that your hearing was deceived;
Do not stoop to such vain hopes as these.
As one prepared long since, courageously,
As becomes one worthy as you were of such a city,
Firmly draw near the window,
And listen with emotion, but not
With the complainings and entreaties of cowards,
Listen, your last enjoyment, to the sounds,
The wonderful instruments of the mystic company,
And say farewell, farewell to Alexandria you are losing.

See Plutarch's *Life of Antony*, § 75 (and Shakespeare's *Anthonie and Cleopatra*, iv. 3). A translation by G. Valassopoulo will be found in E. M. Forster's *Pharos and Pharillon*, p. 46.

27

FINALITIES

In the midst of terror and suspicions,
With mind agitated and frightened eyes,
We make solutions, plan what to do
In order to escape the certain
Danger that so terribly threatens us.
And yet we are mistaken; that is not in our path.
The messages were false—
(Or we didn't hear them, or didn't understand properly).
Another disaster, one we never dreamed of,
Suddenly, tempestuously comes down on us,
And unprepared—no time now—takes us off.

28

IONIC

Because we have broken their statues,
Because we have turned them out of their temples,
They have not died, the gods, for that, at all.
O land of Ionia, you, they love you still,
And you they still remember in their souls.
When an August morning dawns over you
Through your atmosphere passes an ardour from their life;
And sometimes an aerial youthful form,
Indefinite, with swift transition,
Passes upon your hills.

29

SCULPTOR OF TYANA

I'm no beginner, as you've heard from various
People: I've handled quite a lot of stone.
In my own country, Tyana, I'm well-known;
Here too a lot of orders have begun
To come from Senators, for pieces such
As I can show you now.
Look at this *Rhea*,
Venerable, full of strength, ancient. Here you see a
Portrait of *Pompey*. This is *Marius*,
And *Scipio Africanus*, and *Paulus Aemilius*,
As like as I could make them every one.
Patroklus (I must give him another touch).
And that is *Kaesarion*, over there,
Next to those marble fragments rather bilious.

Now for some time I have been occupied
With a *Poseidon*. Specially I've tried
To find a way the horses should be done;
Modelled ever so lightly, so that where
Their bodies and their hoofs you seem to see—
They do not tread the earth, but skim the sea.

This I love best: affection sanctified
My workmanship and greater care refined:
Him, one hot day of summer, when I seemed
To climb to the ideals of the mind,
The *Youthful Hermes* you see here I dreamed.

30

WHAT THINGS ARE DANGEROUS

Said Myrtias (a Syrian student
At Alexandria; in the reign
Of the Emperor Constans and the Emperor Constantius;
In part a Gentile, but of Christian inclination):
"Strengthened by contemplation and study,
I will not fear my passions like a coward.
My body I will give up to pleasures,
To the enjoyments that are dreamed about,
To the more audacious erotic desires,
Lascivious ardours of my blood, without
A single fear, because whenever I will—
And I shall have the will power, fortified
As I shall be by contemplation and study—
At critical moments I shall find again
My spirit as ascetic as before."

Constans and Constantius, sons of Constantine the Great, succeeded him, jointly with their brother Constantine II, on his death in 337. Constantius reigned alone till 361, after the death of his two brothers in 351.

31

THE GLORY OF THE PTOLEMYS

I am the son of Lagos, King. I've won,
With power and wealth, all the domain of pleasure.
Barbarian or Macedonian none can measure
Equal or near me. Seleukos's son
Is comic with his vulgar luxuries.
If you ask more, it is not far to seek.
The mistress city, crown of all things Greek,
In every faculty every art most wise.

Ptolemy I, "Sôtêr" (son of Lagos, a Macedonian of obscure origin, and of Arsinoe, a former mistress of Philip of Macedon), was one of the generals of Alexander the Great, and after his death founded at Alexandria, where he reigned, 323–285 B.C., the Greek dynasty of the Ptolemys. Another general, Seleukos, founded the Seleukid dynasty in Syria.

32

ITHAKA

Setting out on the voyage to Ithaka
You must pray that the way be long,
Full of adventures and experiences.
The Laistrygonians, and the Kyklopes,
Angry Poseidon,—don't be afraid of them;
You will never find such things on your way,
If only your thoughts be high, and a select
Emotion touch your spirit and your body.
The Laistrygonians, the Kyklopes,
Poseidon raging—you will never meet them,
Unless you carry them with you in your soul,
If your soul does not raise them up before you.

You must pray that the way be long;
Many be the summer mornings
When with what pleasure, with what delight
You enter harbours never seen before;
At Phoenician trading stations you must stop,
And must acquire good merchandize,
Mother of pearl and coral, amber and ebony,
And sensuous perfumes of every kind;
As much as you can get of sensuous perfumes;
You must go to many cities of Egypt,
To learn and still to learn from those who know.

You must always have Ithaka in your mind,
Arrival there is your predestination.
But do not hurry the journey at all.
Better that it should last many years;
Be quite old when you anchor at the island,
Rich with all you have gained on the way,
Not expecting Ithaka to give you riches.

Ithaka has given you your lovely journey.
Without Ithaka you would not have set out.
Ithaka has no more to give you now.

Poor though you find it, Ithaka has not cheated you.
Wise as you have become, with all your experience,
You will have understood the meaning of an Ithaka.

The last six lines, translated by G. Valassopoulo, will be found in E. M. Forster's *Pharos and Pharillon*, p. 77.

33

HERODES ATTIKOS

Herôdês Attikos—there's glory for you!

Alexander of Seleukeia, one of our best sophists,
Arriving at Athens to lecture,
Finds the town empty because Herodes
Was in the country. And the young people
Had all followed him there to hear him.
So Alexander the Sophist
Writes a letter to Herodes and
Asks him to send the Greeks back to town.
But subtle Herod answers at once
"I am coming back myself and the Greeks with me."

How many boys in Alexandria now,
In Antioch or in Beirut
(The speakers of tomorrow the Greek world is preparing),
At their rather select tables assembling,
Where the talk is now of the beauties of discussion,
And now about their marvellous love-affairs,
Silently fall silent and absent-minded.
They leave their glasses near them untouched
While they think about the fortune of Herod—
What other sophist was ever thought worthy of this?—
Whatever he wants and whatever he does that
The Greeks (the Greeks of all people!) should follow him,
Not to criticise or to argue,
Not even to pick and choose, but just to follow.

Herodes Atticus, A.D. 101–177, "combined admired eloquence with vast wealth" (H. J. Rose, *Handbook of Grk. Lit.*). See Philostratus, *Vitae Sophist.*, II, 1, and Aulus Gellius, *Noct. Att.*, XIX. 12.

34

PHILHELLENE

Mind the engraving is done artistically.
The expression serious and dignified.
The crown had better be rather narrow;
I don't like those broad Parthian ones.
The inscription in Greek, as usual;
Nothing exaggerated, nothing pompous—
The proconsul might misunderstand it, as
He's always poking about and sending to Rome—
But properly honorific of course.
On the other side something very exquisite;
Some beautiful young athlete throwing the discus.
Above all I charge you to see—
And for God's sake, Sithaspes, don't let them forget—
That after the KING and the SAVIOUR
There be engraved in neat lettering: PHILHELLENE.
Now don't start any of your clever talk,
Your "Where are the Greeks?" and "What Greek can there be
Here behind Zagros, and beyond Phraata?"
So many others, more barbarian than we are,
If they inscribe it, we shall do the same.
And after all don't forget that now and then
There come to us from Syria lecturers,
And versemakers, and other busybodies.
So we are not quite greekless, I believe.

One of the last puppet monarchs of the Seleucid Kingdom in the last century before Christ is supposed to be ordering his coinage. Zagros is a mountain on the confines of Media and Babylonia; Phraata, a city of NW. Media, was the winter residence of the Parthian Kings. See note on no. 50.

35

ALEXANDRIAN KINGS

The Alexandrians came in a crowd
To see the children of Cleopatra,
Kaisarion, and Kaisarion's little brothers,
Alexander and Ptolemy, who for the first
Time were being taken to the Sports Ground
In a wonderful military parade.

Alexander—him they called King of
Armenia, and of Media, and of the Parthians,
Ptolemy—they called him King
Of Kilikia, of Syria, of Phoinikê.
Kaisarion was standing a little forward,
Dressed in pink tinted silk,
On his breast a garland of hyacynths,
His belt a double row of sapphires and amethysts;
His shoes were tied with white ribbons
Embroidered with rosy-coloured pearls.
They called him rather more than the little ones,
Him they called King of Kings.

The Alexandrians understood of course
That this was only words and play acting.

But the day was poetical and warm,
The sky blue, a pale blue,
The Alexandrian Sports Ground a
Triumph of artistic achievement;
The magnificence of the courtiers extraordinary,
Kaisarion all grace and beauty
(Cleopatra's son, blood of the children of Lagos);
The Alexandrians flocked to the festival,
And were enthusiastic, and began to applaud,

In Greek, in Egyptian, and some in Hebrew,
Enchanted with the lovely spectacle—
Although they knew of course what it was worth,
What empty words these Kingships.

The title King of Kings was conferred on Caesarion by Antony in 34 B.C.; see Plutarch's *Life of Antony*, § 54; and Shakespeare's *Anthonie and Cleopatra*, iii. 6. A translation by G. Valassopoulos will be found in E. M. Forster's *Pharos and Pharillon*, p. 78.

36

IN CHURCH

I love the Church—its seraphim with six
Wings, and the silver vessels, and candlesticks,
The pulpit, the eikons, and the burning wicks.

The Church of all the Greeks, and when I enter in,
With smoky fragrance of the incenses,
Liturgical harmony and cadences,
The priests and their majestic presences,
The solemn rhythm of their every movement—
Arrayed in shining vestments on the pavement—
To the great honours of our race my thoughts return,
The glory of our Byzantine achievement.

The words "on the pavement", put in for the rhyme, are not in the original.

37

RETURN

Return often and take me,
Beloved sensation, return and take me—
When the body's memory awakens,
And old desire resurges in the blood;
When the lips and the skin remember,
And the hands feel as if they are touching again.

Return often and take me in the night,
When the lips and the skin remember . . .

38

AS MUCH AS YOU CAN

And if you can't make your life as you like it,
Try this at least
As much as you can: do not cheapen it
In much contact with the world,
In many movements and conversations.

Never cheapen your life by taking it about,
Going around often and exposing it
To communication and intercourse
And their daily silliness,
Until it becomes a sort of tiresome visitor.

39

VERY SELDOM

There is an old man; bent up and exhausted,
Crippled by years and by his own excesses,
Pacing slowly he passes up the alley.
Yet when he goes into his house to hide there
His age and shabbiness, he meditates
The holding he still has in youthfulness.

Young men even now are repeating his verses.
His visions pass before their lively eyes.
Their healthy brains enjoying,
Their welldrawn, tightskinned flesh,
Even now are moved by his revelations of beauty.

40

I WENT

I was not bound. I let myself go completely, went
To those indulgences, half actual,
And half were turned about in my own brain;
Went into the illuminated night;
And drank strong wines, as when
The champions of pleasure drink strong wine.

41

FOR THE SHOP

Carefully, neatly he folded them between
Wrappings of silk, expensive, fine and green.

Rubies like roses, pearls made into lilies,
And amethystine violets. As his will is,

He made, and sees them fair; not as he has known
Or noted nature. In the safe they're thrown,

Proof of his daring workmanship and skill.
A buyer comes into the shop; he'll still

Sell from their cases other pretty things—
Bracelets, and chains, and necklaces and rings.

Homophonously rhymed couplets; cf. nos. 3 and 15.

42

THE GRAVE OF THE GRAMMARIAN LYSIAS

Near the Beirut library, just on the right
As you go in, we buried Lysias the Wise
Grammarian. A very proper site,
Near to the things that even there may live
Still in his memory—notes, texts, technologies,
Scriptures, and volumes of Greek commentaries.
So, going to our books, we'll look and give
Due honour to the grave in which he lies.

43

FAR AWAY

This memory I should like to tell . . .
But it has faded now . . . there is nothing hardly remaining
So far away it lies in my first years of manhood.

A skin as if made of jasmine in the night . . .
That evening of August—was it August? I hardly remember . . .
The eyes now? I think they were blue—Or was it September? . . .
Yes they were blue; as blue as a sapphire's light.

The words "in the night" and "Or was it September" are inserted for the sake of the rhyme and are not in the original.

44

THE GRAVE OF EURION

Within this tomb's elaborate artistries,
Composed entirely of syenite,
Which so many violets cover, so many lilies,
Buried the beautiful Eurion lies.
Twenty-five years old, an Alexandrian,
On his father's side of an old Macedonian clan,
Of a line of officials on his mother's side;
Philosophy with Aristokleitos reading,
With Paros rhetoric, to the sacred writings applied
Himself at Thebes; of the Arsinoite
Nome he wrote a history—that at least still is
With us. But we have lost the more precious delight—
His form, a vision from Apollo proceeding.

The word *alabarches*, translated "official", is used by Josephus as the title of the chief magistrate of the Alexandrian Jews; cf. also Anth. Pal., xi. 383. In Juvenal (i. 130), and Cicero (*Att.*, ii. 17), who applies it sarcastically to Pompey, it appears in the form *arabarches*, meaning apparently a tax collector or officer of customs.

45

CHANDELIER

The four walls of a chamber small and bare
Are hung with curtains plain and green;
There's a fine chandelier; the candles flare,
And in each flame burning there
Is a morbid lust, a lust of passion.

Within that chamber, brightly lighted, small,
From chandelier and candle-sheen
No ordinary light pours down at all,
No bodies ineffectual
Dare to enjoy the conflagration.

46

THEODOTOS

If you are one of the genuinely elect,
Mind how you acquire your domination.
However much you are glorified, your achievements
In Italy and in Thessaly
However much the cities talk about them;
However many decrees of honour
Your admirers may have published in Rome,
Neither your joy nor yet your triumph will endure,
Nor will you feel a superior being—superior indeed!—
When at Alexandria Theodotos brings you,
Upon a bloodstained pan,
The wretched Pompey's head.

Do not repose on the fact that in your life,
Limited, well-ordered, and pedestrian,
There are no spectacular and frightful things like that.
Perhaps this very hour you have a neighbour
And into his well-kept house there goes—
Unseen, not in material shape—Theodotos,
Carrying, just like that, a dreadful head.

See Plutarch's *Life of Pompey*. According to Plutarch Theodotos of Chios, "an hired schoolmaster to teach the young King Rhetoricke", persuaded the Egyptians to kill Pompey when he landed; but it was an unnamed Egyptian, and not Theodotos, who presented the severed head to Caesar.

47

THE WISE OF THINGS AT HAND

> "Now the Gods have perception of things that shall happen, and men of those now coming to pass, but wise men of those things that be just coming along."
>
> Philostratus, *Life of Apollonius of Tyana*, viii. 7

Things that are happening are known by mortals,
And things to come by gods, who are the clear
And only masters of illumination;
Of things to come those that approach the portals
Wise men perceive. Their ear

Sometimes in hours of study most profound
Is troubled; and the strange noises appear
To come to them of things that near their station;
And they attend devoutly. While no sound
Outside street-people hear.

The words "portals" and "station" are not in the original, but have been introduced to keep the pattern of the rhymes.

48

MORNING SEA

Here let me stand. Let me too look at nature a little.
The sea this morning and the cloudless heaven
Their brilliant blue and yellow beach; and all
Beautiful and flooded in light.

Here let me stand. Let me flatter myself I see all this—
(I really did see it for a moment as I first stood here)—
All this and not here too my own imaginings,
My memories, the apparitions of pleasure.

A translation by G. Valassopoulo is given in *Pharos and Pharillon*, p. 76.

49

AT THE CAFÉ ENTRANCE

My attention something they said beside me
Turned towards the entrance of the café.
And I saw the beautiful body which looked
As if Eros himself had made it with his extreme skill—
Modelling with delight the symmetry of his limbs;
Lifting up the sculpture of his figure;
Modelling the face with affection
And leaving from the touch of his own fingers
A feeling on the forehead, on the eyes and on the lips.

50

OROPHERNES

The man who here upon the tetradrachm
Appears to have a smile upon his face,
A smile on a refined and handsome face,
He is Orophernes son of Ariarathes.

A child they turned him out of Cappadocia,
Out of the great palace of his forefathers,
And they sent him away to grow up in
Ionia, and to be forgotten among strangers.

O those wonderful Ionian nights
When fearlessly, and in quite a Greek fashion
He got to know the fullness of pleasure.
Within his heart, always an Asiatic;
But in his manners and his speech a Greek,
With his turquoise ornaments, dressed like a Greek,
His body perfumed with oil of jasmine,
And of the lovely young men of Ionia
Loveliest himself and most idealistic.

Later when the Syrians in Cappadocia
Entered, and made him King,
He threw himself into the Kingship
To enjoy himself a new way every day,
To gather up and snatch at gold and silver,
In order to be gladdened and to brag
At the sight of piles of riches glittering.
As for any thought of the country, or government—
He didn't even know what was going on all round.

The Cappadocians soon threw him out;
And he declined in Syria, in the palace
Of Demetrios, in amusement and laziness.

One day, however, his great idleness
Was interrupted by unaccustomed thoughts;
He remembered that by his mother Antiochis,
And through that ancient dame Stratonike,
He too was connected with the crown of Syria,
And was himself a Seleukid very nearly.
For a little he came out of his lewdness and drinking,
And incompetently and in half bewilderment,
He tried to start something of an intrigue,
To do something, to make some sort of plan,
And he failed miserably and disappeared.

His end must have been recorded somewhere and lost;
Or perhaps history passed over it,
And, justifiably, so insignificant
An incident did not deign to notice.

The man who here upon this tetradrachm
Has left some of the charm of his lovely youth,
A gleam from his poetical beauty,
The sensuous memory of an Ionian boy,
This is Orophernes son of Ariarathes.

See Athenaeus, X, 440 B. Holophernes, a supposititious son of Ariarathes IV, is said to have got possession of the Kingdom of Cappadocia for a short time in 157 B.C. His mother Antiochis was a daughter of Antiochus III, and Stratonike his grandmother, daughter of Antiochus II, Kings of Syria. Sir Maurice Bowra has called my attention to two passages in the second volume of Edwyn Bevan's *House of Seleucus* (1902); p. 157 referring to the youth of Orophernes, and pp. 205–209 to his later history; while plate III shows his head on a coin. There can be little doubt that Bevan's work was the source for this and perhaps for other poems; a sentence on p. 159, for instance, might very well have suggested number 34, *Philhellene*.

51

HE SWEARS

He swears from time to time to
Begin a better life
Whenever though the night comes
With its own counsellings,
With its own compromises,
And its own undertakings;
But whenever the night comes
With its own domination,
Of the body that wills and wants, to that same
Fatal enjoyment, lost, he goes again.

52

REPRESENTATION

My work is in my heart and in my mind.
But slowness of composing now dismays.
The day has too much tried me; for its face
Is ever darkening; always blowing and raining.
To see and not to say I feel inclined.
This is the drawing which I look at now:
Here by the spring I see a lovely boy
Is lying down; suppose he has been running.
A lovely child; and what a heavenly sunning
Of noon has folded him in sleep and joy.
Long time I sit and look, for this is how
After art's toil art rests me and repays.

53

ONE NIGHT

The room was penurious and common,
Hidden over a disreputable tavern,
The alley could be seen from the window,
Unclean and narrow. From below
Came the voices of a few workmen
Who were playing cards and having a good time.

There on the vulgar on the humble bed
I had the body of love, I had the lips,
The sensuous, the rosy lips of wine,
Rosy with such a wine, that even now
Here as I write, after so many years,
In my solitary house, I am drunk again.

54

THE BATTLE OF MAGNESIA

All his old vigour, all his courage lost,
His body now tired out and ill almost

Must be his only care. Through what remains
Of life he'll bear no burdens. So maintains

Philip at least; tonight he's playing dice
And wants amusement. "Roses would be nice,

"Lots, on the table! Antiochus may
Be smashed. So what? Magnesia, they say,

"Annihilated his grand host. They do
Exaggerate. It cannot all be true—

We hope! No friend, he's still our kin. For such
One hope is quite enough—perhaps too much."

Philip of course will not put off the feast.
However hard his life has been, at least

One quality remains; a mind well kept
Remembers just how long the Syrians wept

When mother Macedonia went down fighting.
"To dinner! Slaves! The music, and the lighting!"

Philip, the last king of Macedonia of that name, had been defeated by the Romans at Kynoskefalai in 197 B.C., and lost his throne. Seven years later Antiochus the Great, King of Syria, was defeated by the Romans at the battle of Magnesia.

55

MANUEL KOMNENOS

The King and Emperor Manuel Komnenos
One melancholy morning in September
Felt death was near him. The astrologers
(The paid ones) of the court were babbling
That he still had many more years to live.
Yet while they were still talking, himself
Calling to mind old habits of piety,
Gives orders from the monastery cells
Ecclesiastical vestments should be brought,
And puts them on; and is glad to show forth
The solemn mien of a priest or a monk.

Blessed are they all who believe,
And like the Emperor Manuel end their days
Dressed in the solemn vesture of their faith.

Manuel I, Komnenos, Emperor of Byzantium A.D. 1143–1180, had been defeated by the Turks at Myriokefalon in 1176. For this incident, see Nicetas Choniates (Bonn, 1835), p. 288.

56

THE DISPLEASURE OF SELEUKIDES

Demetrios was displeased, Demetrios
Seleukides, to learn that in Italy
A Ptolemy had arrived in such a state—
With only three or four servants,
Badly dressed and on foot. Figures of fun
They will come to be, a laughing-stock in Rome
Their whole family. That really they have become
Of course a sort of servants of the Romans
Seleukides well knows; for that they give them
And that they take away their thrones from them
Arbitrarily, as they desire, he knows.
But at least in their appearance
They might keep up some sort of dignity;
They should not forget that they are kings still,
That they are still called (alas!) kings.

Hence the vexation of the Seleukid
Demetrios; and at once he offered Ptolemy
Robes all of purple, and a splendid crown,
Some very costly diamonds, a number of
Attendants and followers, and his most expensive horses,
That he might make his appearance in Rome properly,
As an Alexandrian Greek monarch.
But the son of Lagos, who had come to beg,
Knew his own business and refused them all;
He had no need of these luxuries at all.

This Demetrios is Demetrios Soter, son of Seleukos IV and grandson of Antiochos the Great, who spent his youth in Rome as a hostage, and reigned in Syria 162–150 B.C. The Ptolemy is Ptolemy VI, Philometor, who, having been expelled from Alexandria by his brother, visited Rome in 164 B.C. and asked the Senate to reinstate him. See Diodorus Siculus, XXXI, 18; and Polybius, XXXI, 11 ff. See also no. 80, which refers to an imaginary incident in the same brotherly dispute; and Bevan's *House of Seleucus*, vol. II, p. 189.

In old clothes, humbly he came into Rome,
And lodged at the house of a small craftsman.
Then he presented himself as an unfortunate,
And as a poor man before the Senate,
That he might come with more effect a-begging.

57

IN THE STREET

His quite attractive face a little pale;
His brown eyes as if dazzled;
Twenty-five years old, but looks more like twenty;
With something rather artistic in his dress,
Some colour of his tie, and shape of collar—
Aimlessly he walks along the street,
Still as if hypnotised by the lawless pleasure,
The very lawless pleasure has been his.

58

WHEN THEY AWAKEN

Try to keep them, Poet,
However few there be that can be stayed,
The visions of your loving.
Put them half hidden in your sentences;
Try to hold them, Poet,
When they awaken in your brain
In the night-time, or in the brightness of mid-day.

59

BEFORE THE STATUE OF ENDYMION

Four mules, all white, with silver decorations,
Draw me, to Latmos in a chariot white
Come from Miletos, sailing for this rite,
Endymion's sacrifices and libations,
An Alexandrian ship with purple dight.
Here is the statue. In ecstasy I gaze
On fair Endymion whom all men praise.
My slaves bring jasmine baskets; acclamations
Wake the auspicious joy of ancient days.

60

GREY

Looking at an opal a half grey opal
I remembered two beautiful grey eyes
I had seen it must have been twenty years before . . .

. . . .

For a month we loved each other.
Then he went away, I think to Smyrna,
To work there; we never saw each other again.

The grey eyes—if he lives—have lost their beauty;
The beautiful face will have been spoiled.

O Memory, preserve them as they were.
And, Memory, all you can of this love of mine
Whatever you can bring back to me tonight.

61

IN A TOWN OF OSROÊNE

Home from the tavern brawl they brought him wounded
Our friend Remon yesterday about midnight.
We left the windows wide open, and bright
On the bed his body was shining in the moonlight.

Medes, Syrians, Greeks, Armenians, we're a mixed pack.
Remon is that sort too. But when shining
We saw his countenance yesterday in the moonlight,
Our thoughts to Plato's Charmides went back.

62

ONE OF THEIR GODS

When one of them was passing through the market
Of Seleukeia, about the hour of evenfall,
Like a tall, a beautiful, a perfect youth,
With the joy of incorruptibility in his eyes,
With his black and perfumed hair,
The passers-by would look at him,
And one would ask another if he knew him,
And if he was a Greek of Syria, or a stranger. But a few
Who observed with greater attention
Would understand and draw aside;
And while he disappeared under the arcades,
In the shadows and in the lights of evening,
Going towards the quarter which at night only
Lives, with orgies and debauchery,
And every kind of drunkenness and lust,
They would wonder which it could be of Them,
And for what disreputable sensuality
He had come down into the streets of Seleukeia
From those Majestical, All-holy Mansions.

63

TOMB OF IASES

Iases here I lie. To whom this proud
City for youth and beauty gave much fame.
The learned wise admired me, and the crowd
Of simpletons. From both I had the same

Joy. But the Hermes and Narcissus fashion
Wasted and killed me. Traveller, you will not blame,
If Alexandrian. You know the passion
Of our life here, the pleasure and the flame.

The literal translation in line 5 is "The fact that the world overmuch regarded me as a Narcissus and a Hermes".

64

TRANSIT

The schoolboy's timid fancies are displayed
Open before him; all night having strayed
Lets himself go; and feeling (our art's due)
His blood so warm and new
Delights in pleasure. Over his body brims
Lawless intoxication, and to love his limbs
Youthfully yield.

Now worthy of our view
Becomes a simple child, a moment through
The High Domain of Poesy passes too
That simple child with blood so warm and new.

65

AT EVENING

Anyhow it wouldn't have lasted long.
The years have shown me that. All the same it was
Stopped rather suddenly when Fate came along.
The lovely life was short.
But how those scents were strong,
On what a wonderful couch we laid ourselves,
And with what pleasures we arrayed ourselves.

An echo from the days of pleasure,
An echo of those days came near me,
I took a letter in my hands, a brand flung
From the flame when we were both young;
I read it again and again till the light failed.

And I went out sadly on to the balcony—
Went out to change my thoughts if only by seeing
A little of the city I loved,
A little movement in the street and shops.

66

FOR AMMONES, WHO DIED AGED 29 IN 610

They want some verses from you, Rafael,
For the poet Ammones, to put on his grave.
Do something in good taste—you can—and something
suave.
You are the very man to write something fitting
For Ammones the poet, who was one of us.

Of course you'll speak about his work—but do
Say something for his beauty too,
That delicate beauty that we loved.

Your Greek is always good and musical.
This time we want all of your mastery.
Into a foreign tongue go our grief and our love as well.
Pour your Egyptian sentiment into the foreign tongue.

Your verses must be written, Rafael,
So that they hold, you know, some of our life,
So that the rhythm and every phrase may tell
An Alexandrian is writing of an Alexandrian.

67

IN THE MONTH OF ATHYR

I read with difficulty
upon the ancient stone
"O LO(RD) JESUS CHRIST."
I can make out a "SO(U)L".
"IN THE MO(NTH) OF ATHYR"
"LEVKI(OS) FELL AS(LEE)P."
At the mention of his age
"He LI(VE)D" so many "YEARS"
The Kappa Zeta means
quite young he fell asleep.
In the damaged part I see
"HI(M) . . . ALEXANDRIAN."
Then there are three more lines
very much mutilated;
But I make out some words
like "OVR T(E)ARS", and "SORROW",
Afterwards "TEARS" again,
and "OF H(IS) GRIEVING (FR)IENDS".
I see that Levkios
had friends whose love was deep.
In the month of Athyr
Levkios fell asleep.

"Kappa Zeta" (KZ) are the Greek numerals for 27. For a translation by G. Valassopoulo, see *Pharos and Pharillon*, p. 79. From this translation I have (consciously) borrowed two words in line 6; and from E. M. Forster's note on the same page may be borrowed the information that the month of Athyr is "the ancient Egyptian November".

68

THE TOMB OF IGNATIOS

Here I am not that Kleon who was talked about
In Alexandria (where it is difficult to impress them)
For my splendid houses, for my gardens,
And for my horses and my carriages,
For the diamonds and the silks I used to wear.
Nay: here am I not that Kleon;
Let his eight and twenty years be blotted out.
I am Ignatios, a lay-reader, who very late
Came to myself; even so ten happy months I lived
In the tranquillity and in the safety of Christ.

Mr. T. Malanos in a note on this poem published in the second volume of his collected critical works (Alexandria, 1943) points out that it is inspired or suggested by four separate passages in the *Lausiac History* of Palladius.

69

SO MUCH I GAZED

So much I gazed on beauty gazing
My vision is full of it full of beauty.

Lines of the body. Red lips. Sensuous limbs.
Such hair, as if taken from Greek statues,
Beautiful always, even when uncombed,
And it falls a little over a white forehead.
Faces of love, just as my poesy
Wanted them . . . in the night-times of my youth,
In the nights of my secret encountering.

70

DAYS OF 1903

I never found them again—so quickly lost . . .
The poetical eyes, the pale,
Pale face . . . darkling in the street . . .

I never found them any more—quite by chance they were
mine,
And I gave them up so easily;
And afterwards agonisingly wanted them.
The poetical eyes, the pale face,
Those lips I never found them any more.

71

THE TOBACCO-SHOP WINDOW

Near the brightly-lit shop window
Of a tobacco-shop they were standing, among many
others.
Then it happened that their glances met,
And the unlawful desire of their flesh
Was timidly, hesitatingly, expressed.
Afterwards uneasily a few steps on the pavement—
Until they smiled, and slightly gave a nod.

And then of course the closed cab . . .
The sensuous nearness of their bodies, with
Hands joined, and joined their lips.

72

TO PLEASURE

Delight and perfume of my life the memory of the hours
When I found and when I held pleasure as I wanted it.
Delight and perfume of my life for me, that I rejected
Every indulgence in habitual loves.

73

KAISARION

Partly to pass the time indeed,
Partly to verify a period's descriptions,
Last night I picked up and began to read
A volume of Ptolemaic inscriptions.
The fulsome praises and the flatteries
Are all alike. Glory to glory succeeds,
All famous, strong, and full of noble deeds;
Their every enterprise the top of wisdom,
As for the women of the house, the same
Each Berenice's, each Kleopatra's fame.

When I had verified my memory of the period
I would have dropped the book, if a small
And unimportant mention of King Kaisarion
Had not immediately drawn my attention . . .

Ah, there you come with your indefinite
Enchantment. In the history a few
Only are the lines to be found about you,
So I have fashioned you more freely in my mind.
I have fashioned you beautiful and sensuous.

My art gives to your countenance
A dreamlike and attractive loveliness.
And so completely have I imagined you,

For Kaisarion (Caesarion) supposed to be the son of Cleopatra by Julius Caesar, see no. 35 above, and the references in Plutarch's Lives of Julius Caesar and Antonius. "As Caesar was determining with himselfe what he should do, Arrius said unto him:

Too many Caesars is not good.

Alluding unto a certaine verse of Homer [*Iliad*, II, 204], that saith:

Too many Lords doth not well.

Therefore Caesar did put Caesarion to death after the death of his mother Cleopatra." North's *Plutarch* (1631), p. 947.

That yesterday late in the night, when my lamp
Was going out—I let it go out on purpose—
I thought you came into my room,
You seemed to stand before me as you must have been
In Alexandria when it was conquered,
Pale and tired, idealistic in your grief,
Still hoping that they would have mercy on you,
The baser sort—chattering their "Too many Cæsars."

74

AT THE HARBOUR

A Tenian ship brought Emes, at the age
Of twenty-eight, to this small anchorage
In Syria, to learn the incense-trade.
He sickened on the voyage; and here conveyed
He died as soon as he was put ashore;
Was poorly buried. A few hours before
Whispered of "home", of his "old parents" too.
But who they were nobody ever knew,
Nor what his town was in the great world of Greece.
It is the lesser ill:
While in this little port he lies at peace,
His parents hope that he is living still.

75

BODY, REMEMBER . . .

Body, remember not how much you have been loved
Only; not only beds where you have lain;
But also those desires that for you
Would shine openly in the eyes,
Would tremble in the voice—and only
A chance impediment brought them to nothing.
For now that all of them are in the past
It is almost as if to those desires
You had given yourself—how they used to shine,
Remember, in the eyes that looked at you,
And how they used to tremble in the voice, for you,
remember.

76

THE TOMB OF LANÊS

The Lanês whom you loved is not here, Marcus, in the tomb,
Here where you come and weep and here remain for hours and
hours.
The Lanês whom you loved so much you have him nearer to
you
When in your house you shut yourself and look upon his
picture,
The picture which has somehow kept what was most precious
in him,
The picture which has somehow kept whatever made you love
him.

Do you remember, Marcus, how you once brought from the
palace
Of the proconsul that most famous painter from Kyrene,
And with what cleverness and craft the man artistically
The minute that he saw your friend he wanted to persuade you
That he must really do him as Hyákinthos, absolutely,
(Of course in that way there would be more talk about his
painting).

Your Lanês in that sort of way was not lending his beauty;
Firmly opposing him he told him he must represent here
Not Hyákinthos, not at all, nor anyone else either,
Only Lánes, son of Rametichos, of Alexandria.

77

NERO'S TERM

Nero was not uneasy when he heard
The answer of the Delfick oracle:
"That he should fear seventy years and three."
He had plenty of time still to enjoy.
He was thirty years old. Quite long enough
Is the appointed term the god allows him
To see about the dangers yet to come.

He will be going back to Rome now a little tired,
But marvellously tired after this journey,
Which was nothing but days of pleasure—
In the theatres, in the gardens, in the sports
grounds . . .
The evening hours in Achaian towns . . .
And better still the joy of naked bodies . . .

So Nero thought. And in Spain Galba
Assembles secretly and drills his army,
The old man Galba, seventy-three years old.

See Suetonius, *Life of Nero*, c. XL.

78

THE NEXT TABLE

He must be hardly twenty-two. And yet
I'm sure that nearly as many years ago
That was the very body I enjoyed.

It isn't a kindling of desire at all.
I only came into the casino a minute ago;
I haven't even had time to drink much.
That very same body I have enjoyed.

If I don't remember where—one thing forgotten
doesn't signify.

There, now that he has sat down at the next table,
I know every movement he makes—and under his
clothes
Naked I can see again the limbs I loved.

79

PERCEPTION

The years of my youth, my life of pleasure—
How clearly I see the meaning of them now.

What unnecessary, what vain repentances . . .

But I did not see the meaning then.

Under the dissolute living of my youth
Were being formed the intentions of my poetry,
The province of my art was being planned.

And that is why my repentances were never lasting.
My resolutions to control myself, to change,
Used to endure for two weeks at most.

80

SINCE FROM ALEXANDRIA

At Delphi for ages they never had seen such beautiful things
As the gifts that were sent by the two rival brothers and kings,
The two Ptolemys. Nevertheless all the priests when they got
The presents, were very uneasy about the response. For a lot
Of skill would be needed, and subtly the answer would have to
be blended,
Deciding of two such great claimants which one should be
rightly offended.
So secretly all through the night they continue their sessions,
Discuss the descendants of Lagos, the family claims and posses-
sions.

But here are the envoys returning. And now they take leave.
They're returning to Egypt, they say. They don't want to
receive
Any oracle-answer at all. The priests are exceedingly glad
At the news; (for of course they will keep all the wonderful
presents they had).
But still they are sorely bewildered. They can't comprehend
The sudden indifference the envoys display: what can it portend?
They don't know that yesterday serious news came to hand.
The response has been given in Rome: that is where they've
divided the land.

The dispute between Ptolemy VI, "Philometor", and his younger brother Ptolemy VII, "Euergetes II" (who succeeded him after his death in 146), took place in 164 B.C., and is referred to in no. 56 above. There seems to be no historical authority for the suggestion that the brothers referred the quarrel to the oracle at Delphi before it was decided for them by Rome.

81

SINCE NINE O'CLOCK

Half past twelve. Quickly the time has passed
Since nine o'clock when I lit the lamp,
And sat down here. I sat here without reading,
And without talking. With whom should I talk
All alone in this house.

The image of my young body,
From nine o'clock when I lit the lamp,
Came and found me and reminded me
Of closed and scented rooms,
Of past pleasure—and pleasure's venturing.
It also brought before my eyes
Streets which have now become unrecognisable,
Centres full of movement which have vanished,
And cafés there were once and theatres.

The image of my young body
Came and brought me the sad things as well;
Family sorrows, separations,
Sentiments of my own people, sentiments
So little appreciated of the dead.

Half past twelve. How the hours have passed.
Half past twelve. How the years have passed.

82

ARISTOBOULOS

The Palace is weeping, the King is weeping,
King Herod mourns and will not be comforted,
The whole city weeps for Artistoboulos
So undeservedly was drowned, by accident
Playing with his friends in the water.

And when they hear about it too in the other parts,
When up in Syria it gets about,
Many of the Greeks also will be grieved;
As many as be poets and sculptors will mourn,
Because Aristoboulos had become known to them;
And what imagination of theirs for any youth
Had ever reached such beauty as this boy's;
What statue of a god thought Antioch as fine
As this one boy of Israel?

She is mourning and weeping, the First Princess,
His mother, chiefest of the Jewish women.
Mourning and weeping the disaster is Alexandra.—
But when she is alone her grief changes.
She groans; she raves; she scolds; she curses.
How they have tricked her! How they have swindled her!
How their purpose at last has come to pass!
They have laid waste the Asmonaean house,
How has the wicked King attained his end,
The treacherous, the base, the sinful King.

How has he gained his end! What an infernal plot
That even Mariamne should notice nothing!
If Mariamne had noticed, if she had suspected,
She would have found a way to save her brother;
She is Queen after all, she could have done something.

How they will be triumphing now and rejoicing secretly
Those spiteful ones, Kypros and Salome;
Those common women, Kypros and Salome.—
And that she should be powerless, and obliged
To pretend that she believes their lies;
That she should not be able to go to the people,
To go out and to call aloud to the Jews,
And tell them, tell them that there's murder done.

See Josephus, *Jewish War*, I, 437 ff.; and *Antiquities*, XV, 2 and 3. Malanos also refers to Renan, *Histoire d'Israel*, vol. V, bk. X, ch. 5. Herod the Great unwillingly made Aristoboulos, brother of his wife Mariamne, high priest when he was only seventeen, but a few months later had him "accidentally" drowned in a bathing-pool, 35 B.C. Kypros was Herod's mother, and Salome his sister. Alexandra, Herod's mother-in-law, mother of his wife Mariamne and of Aristoboulos, was on friendly terms with Cleopatra and tried to interest Antony in the fortunes of her children who were both exceptionally beautiful.

83

UNDER THE HOUSE

Yesterday walking in a quarter
Rather remote, I passed under the house
I used to enter when I was very young.
There on my body Love had taken hold
With his marvellous strength.
And yesterday
When I passed along the old street
Immediately beautified by the magic of love
The shops, the pavements and the stones,
And walls, and balconies, and windows,
Nothing left there was ugly.

As I was standing and looking at the door,
And standing, and lingering under the house,
My whole subsistence began to give back
The sensuous emotion it had stored.

84

AIMILIANOS MONAÊ, ALEXANDRIAN

A.D. 628–655

With countenance and words and ways
A special panoply I'll make;
And, when the wicked men I face,
With fear or weakness never quake.

They'll want to hurt me. No one though,
Of all who have approached and seen me,
My wounds and tender parts will know,
Under the falsities which screen me.

So boasted Aemilianus Monaê.
And did he ever make this armour strong?
In any case he did not wear it long.
Aged twenty-seven, he died in Sicily.

The rhyme fades away in the last stanza, as in the translation.

85

OF THE HEBREWS

A.D. 50

Painter and poet, runner, thrower of the discus,
Fair as Endymion, Ianthes son of Antonios.
From a family dear to the synagogue.

"My most precious days are those
When I leave the search for sensation,
Abandon the hard and beautiful rule of the Greeks,
With their dominant devotion
To white limbs perfectly made and corruptible;
When I become one I should wish
Always to remain; a son of Hebrews, of the holy
Hebrews——"

But he did not remain anything of the sort.
The Hedonism and the Art of Alexandria
Found in him a most assiduous votary.

86

TO REMAIN

It must have been one o'clock at night,
Or half past one.
                    In a corner of the wine shop;
Behind the wooden partition.
Except the two of us the shop quite empty.
A paraffin lamp hardly lighted it.
The waiter who had to sit up was asleep at the door.

No one would have seen us. But anyhow
We had become so excited
We were incapable of precautions.

Our clothes had been half opened—they were not
    many
For a divine month of July was blazing.

Enjoyment of the flesh in the middle
Of our half-opened clothes;
Quick baring of the flesh—and the vision of it
Has passed over twenty-six years; and now has come
Here in these verses to remain.

87

IMENOS

"... Should be loved still more
The pleasure which is procured morbidly and with
corruption;
Rarely finding the body which feels as it would wish—
Which morbidly and with corruption lends
An erotic intensity, unknown to health ..."

Extract from a letter
Of young Imenos (of patrician family) notorious
At Syracuse for his profligacy,
In the profligate times of the third Michael.

"The third Michael" is presumably the Byzantine Emperor Michael III, called "the Drunkard", of the Amorian dynasty, who reigned A.D. 842–867.

88

ON BOARD SHIP

Of course it is like him, this little
Drawing of him in pencil.

Quickly done, on the deck of the ship;
An enchanting afternoon.
The Ionian ocean all around us.

It is like him. But I remember him as better looking,
He was sensitive to the point of morbidness,
And that illuminated his expression.
Better looking he appears to me
Now that my mind recalls him, out of Time.

Out of Time. All these things are very old—
The sketch, and the ship, and the afternoon.

89

OF DEMETRIOS SÔTÊR

162–150 B.C.

Every expectation of his turned out wrong!

He used to imagine he would do famous deeds,
End the humiliation from the time of the battle
Of Magnesia oppressed his country.
Syria should become a strong power again,
With her armies, and with her fleets,
With the great fortresses, and with riches.

He used to suffer, he grieved bitterly in Rome
When he understood in the conversation of his friends,
Young people of the great houses,
With all the delicacy and the politeness
Which they showed to him, to the son
Of King Seleukos Philopator—
When he understood that none the less there was always a secret
Contempt for the dynasties which favoured Greece;
Which had fallen off, which were not for serious work,
Quite unfitted for the leadership of peoples.
He would retire alone, and grow indignant, and swear
That it should not be at all as they thought;
See that he has a will of his own;
He would struggle, and do, and he would uplift.

Only to find a way to get to the East,
To succeed in escaping from Italy—
And all that strength he has
Within his soul, all that energy
Of his he will communicate to the people.

Only to find himself in Syria!
So young he left his country

That he remembered its appearance obscurely.
But in his thoughts he always dwelt on it
As something holy which you approach with adoration,
Like a vision of a lovely place, like a spectacle
Of Greek cities and harbours.—

And now?
Now desperation and grief.
The boys in Rome were right.
It is not possible for the dynasties to endure
That came out of the Macedonian Occupation.

No matter: he had striven himself,
He had struggled as much as he could.
And in his black disenchantment,
He now takes only one thing into account
With pride; that even in his unsuccess
He shows the world the same unsubject courage.

Everything else—they were dreams and labours in vain.
Even Syria—it is hardly like his own country;
It is the land of Herakleides and of Balas.

Demetrius, called "Sôtêr" (Saviour), son of Seleucus IV "Philopator", grandson of Antiochus the Great, was brought up in Rome as a hostage. At the age of twenty-three he succeeded in escaping, and regained the throne of Syria with Roman recognition. He expelled the Satrap Herakleides from Babylon, but was afterwards defeated by the adventurer Alexander Balas. See also no. 56, and Bevan, *House of Seleucus*, vol. II, pp. 188 ff.

90

THE AFTERNOON SUN

This room, how well I know it.
Now they are rented this one and the next
As business offices. The whole house has become
Offices for agents, and merchants, and Companies.

O how familiar it is, this room.

Near the door just here there was the sofa,
And in front of it a Turkish carpet;
Close by the shelf with two yellow vases.
On the right; no, opposite, a wardrobe with a mirror.
In the middle a table where he used to write;
And the three big wicker chairs.
At the side of the window was the bed
Where we made love so many times.

They must still be somewhere the poor old things.

At the side of the window was the bed;
The afternoon sun fell on it half-way up.

. . . One afternoon at four o'clock, we parted
Only for a week . . . Alas,
That week became perpetual.

91

IF DEAD INDEED

"Whither withdrawn, where was the Wise One lost?
After his many miracles,
After the reputation of his teaching
Which to so many nations spread about
He was hidden suddenly and no man learned
With definiteness what became of him
(Neither has anyone ever seen his grave).
Some put it out that he had died at Ephesus.
But Damis never wrote it; nothing
About Apollonios dying Damis ever wrote.
Others have said he disappeared at Lindos.
Or it may be that that account
Is true, that he was taken up in Crete,
At the ancient sanctuary of Diktynna.—
And yet again we have his miraculous,
His supernatural appearance
To a certain young student at Tyana.—
Perhaps the time has not come for him to return
To be manifested to the world again;
Or having been transformed, perhaps, among us
He goes about unrecognised.—But he will reappear
As he was, teaching the right; and then of course
He will bring back the worship of our gods,
And our classical Grecian ceremonies."

So mused in his poor dwelling—
After a reading of Philostratos
Concerning Apollonios of Tyana—
One of the few pagans, the very few
Who had remained. Moreover—an insignificant
Man and timorous—to all appearance
He played the Christian and even went to church
himself.

It was the period in which reigned
With his extreme devotion, the elder Justin,
And Alexandria, a god-fearing city,
Abhorred all miserable idolaters.

Apollonius of Tyana (in Cappadocia), born 4 B.C., was a Pythagorean philosopher who enjoyed wide fame for his ascetic life, his virtuous teaching, his travels, and his supposed miracles. His *Life* was written by the "sophist" or itinerant lecturer Philostratus, born in Lemnos about A.D. 172, at the request of Julia Domna, wife of the Roman Emperor Severus, and is said by the writer to be based partly on the memoirs of an Assyrian disciple of Apollonius named Damis. The words of the heading "If he did actually die" are taken from the work of Philostratus (bk. VIII, ch. 29), and the following chapters give the various stories of his death here referred to.

Justin I was made emperor in A.D. 518 and died in 527 when he was succeeded by his nephew Justinian; he was called "The Elder" to distinguish him from Justinian's nephew and successor, Justin II (A.D. 565–578).

The word translated "classical", in line 24, means literally "in good taste".

92

ANNA COMNENA

Anna Comnena, in her *Alexiad's* prelude,
Makes lamentation for her widowhood.

Her soul is in a whirl of dizziness. "And
With rivers of tears", she tells us, "I bedew
My eyes . . . Woe for the tempests" of her life,
"Woe for the revolutions." Sorrow burns her
"To the bones and to the marrow and to the cleaving of
her soul."

It is more like the truth that only one sorrow
One mortal sorrow this ambitious woman knew;
Only one deep hurt she had
(Even if she never confesses it) this haughty Greek,
That she never managed, with all her cleverness,
To seize the Empire; but it was taken
Almost out of her hands by the insolent John.

The *Alexiad*, the life of the Byzantine Emperor Alexios I Comnenos (1081–1118), was written by his learned daughter Anna. He was succeeded by his capable son John II (1118–1143), and when Anna tried to rebel against her brother she was not supported by her husband, Nikeforos Bryennios. The quotations describing her grief on her husband's death in 1137, when she retired into a monastery and took to literature, are all taken from ch. iv of the prologue to the *Alexiad* (ed. Reifferscheid, vol. I, pp. 7, 8).

Only the first two lines are rhymed.

The word "insolent" or "impetuous" in the Greek seems to be taken from the Byzantine historian Nicetas Choniates (Bonn, p. 8), who says that the eldest son John was his father's favourite, but Anna was the favourite of her mother, who accused John of being, among other things, "impetuous".

93

SHADOWS COME

One candle is enough.
Because its obscure light
Better agrees, will give
A more concordant gloom
When the Shadows come,
The Shadows come of Love.

One candle is enough.
Let the room tonight
Not have a lot of light.
So wholly in a muse,
And only in supposing,
And with the little light—
So now within a muse
A vision I'll invite
And let the Shadows come,
The Shadows come of Love.

94

YOUNG MEN OF SIDON

A.D. 400

The actor they had brought to entertain them
Recited some epigrams, an exquisite choice.

The drawing-room opened on to the garden;
And from the flowers came a delicate fragrance
Combining with the perfumes of the boys,
Of the five scented young Sidonians.

Meleager, Krinagoras, Rianos were read.
But when the actor said,
"Athenian Aeschylus son of Euphorion here"—
(Perhaps with too pronounced significance
Reciting the "tried valour", the "Marathonian grove"),
A lively youth, literary-fanatical,
Jumped up at once, and cried:

"Oh but I don't like that quatrain at all.
Such phrases always seem somehow faint-hearted.
Give to your work—I preach—give all your power,
And all your thought, and again in the hour
Of trial think of your work, even when the time so late is—
That is what I expect of you, that is my call.

Five lines in the introductory part of this poem are left unrhymed: the rest is rhymed in an elaborate pattern reproduced in the translation.

The epitaph on Aeschylus may be found among the fragments of Aeschylus (Wecklein, 495; Loeb Classics, *Aeschylus*, Doubtful or Spurious Fragments, no. 272; vol. 2, p. 520); or in Mackail's *Select Epigrams from the Greek Anthology*, p. 153. It is doubtful whether the epitaph was written by Aeschylus himself; it is remarkable because it says nothing about his works, but records only the fact that he fought against the Persians at Marathon, where the army of Darius, under the command of Datis and Artaphernes, was defeated in 490 B.C., and it implies that militant patriotism is more important that poetry. This attitude is denounced as "faint-hearted" by the "literary-fanatical" and scented young Sidonian.

Not to put altogether out of your head
Tragedy's bright Argument—who need recall
An Agamemnon or Prometheus magical,
A presence to Orestes, to Cassandra imparted,
Or Seven Against Thebes?—not for your memorial instead
To say only that in the soldiers' stand-and-fall
You too battled with Artafernes and with Datis."

95

DARIUS

Fernazes the poet on the serious part
Of his epic poem is now at work.
How that the kingdom of the Persians
Was taken over by Darius son of Hystaspes. (From him
Is descended our own glorious monarch
Mithridates, called Dionysos and Eupator). At this point
Philosophy is called for; he must analyse
The feelings which Darius must have had;
Arrogance perhaps and intoxication? No—rather
A sort of understanding of the vanity of greatness.
Upon this point the poet deeply meditates.

But his servant interrupts him who comes
Running in, and announces the momentous news.
The war with the Romans has begun.
The greater part of our army has crossed the frontiers.

The poet is dumbfounded. What a disaster!
How ever could our glorious monarch now,
Could Mithridates, Dionysos and Eupator,
Give any of his attention to Greek poems?—
To Greek poems, just fancy, in the midst of war!

Fernazes is worried. How unfortunate!
Just as he had it in his grasp with his "*Dareios*"
Positively to distinguish himself, and his critics
His envious critics, once and for all to shut them up!
What a putting-off, what a putting-off of all his plans!

And if it were only a hold-up, well and good.
But let us see if we are even safe
Here in Amisos. It isn't a particularly strong town,
The Romans are most frightful enemies.

Can we ever bring it off with them,
We Cappadocians? Can it ever come to pass?
Can we be now a match for the legions?
Great gods, defenders of Asia, help us now.—

None the less in all his trouble and commotion,
Insistently still the poetic notion comes and goes—
Most likely of course arrogance and intoxication;
Arrogance and intoxication must have filled Darius.

Mithridates IV, the Great, called also Dionysos and Eupator, King of Pontus, 120–63 B.C.

96

A BYZANTINE NOBLEMAN IN EXILE WRITING VERSES

Those who are frivolous themselves may call me
Frivolous. In serious matters I was always most
Attentive. I am ready to insist
That no one is more familiar than I am
With Fathers or Scriptures or Conciliar Canons.
Whenever he was in doubt, Botaneiates,
In any ecclesiastical difficulty,
Used to consult me, and me first of all.
But banished here, (let her look to it, the malicious
Eirene Doukaina), where afflictions gall me,
It is not strange if I amuse myself
Making my six or eight verses—or if it enthral me
To make mythological stories
Of Hermes, and of Dionysos, and of Apollo,
Of Thessalian and Peloponnesian heroes; and I follow
The strictest rules composing my iambics,
Such as—allow me to say—the literary men
Of Constantinople don't know how to write.
Probably my very correctness provokes their censure.

The nobleman is probably Michael VII, called "Parapinakes", "a surname which denotes the reproach which he shared with an avaricious favourite who enhanced the price, and diminished the measure, of wheat", says Gibbon, who adds that "his character was degraded, rather than ennobled, by the virtues of a monk and the learning of a sophist". He was forced to abdicate in 1078 by Nikeforos III Botaniates; Nikeforos was himself dethroned in 1081 by Alexios I Comnenos, who had married Eirene of the Doukas family (Doukaina).

97

FAVOUR OF ALEXANDER BALAS

O, I don't mind that my chariot broke a wheel,
And I lost a ridiculous race. With some good wine,
And lots of lovely roses I will steal
The hours of night. All Antioch is mine,
Giving to none more glory than to me.
I am Balas's weakness, his idolatry.
Tomorrow they'll say that the race was unfair, you'll see.
(But if I had told them privately—if I had the bad taste—
Even my one wheeled car would have been first-placed).

Alexander Balas was an adventurer who overthrew Demetrios I, Soter, and reigned in Syria 150–146 B.C.

98

I BROUGHT TO ART

I sit and meditate.
Desires and sensations
I brought to my Art—
Some things half-seen,
Faces or lines;
And of imperfect loves
Some memories unsure.
Let me give myself up to it.
It knows how to fashion
A Form of Beauty;
Almost imperceptibly
My life completing,
Impressions combining,
And combining the days.

99

THEIR BEGINNING

The consummation of their lawless pleasure
Was done. They rose up from the mattress;
Hurriedly dressed themselves without speaking.
They go out separately, secretly from the house; and as
They walk rather uneasily up the street, it seems
As if they suspect that something about them betrays
On what sort of bed they lay down not long ago.

But for the artist how his life has gained.
Tomorrow, the next day or years after will be written
The lines of strength that here had their beginning.

DEMARATOS

The theme, a Character of Demaratos,
Proposed by Porphyry, in conversation,
Was thus expressed by the young sophist
(Intending later a rhetorical development).

"At first of King Darius, and afterwards
The courtier of King Xerxes :
At present with Xerxes and his expedition,
Now at last Demaratos will be justified.

"A great injustice has been done to him.
He was the son of Ariston. Shamelessly
His enemies had bribed the oracle.
And it was not enough that they had deprived him of
 the Kingship,
But when he had submitted, and resolved
To live with patience as a private citizen,
They had to insult him before the people as well,
They had publicly to humiliate him at the festival.

"Wherefore he serves Xerxes most zealously.
With the great Persian army,
Himself too will return again to Sparta;
And King as before, how he will turn him out
Immediately, how he will put him to shame
That scoundrel Leotychides.

And his days go by full of anxiety;
Giving advice to the Persians, explaining to them
What they must do in order to conquer Greece.

"Many cares, much thinking and therefore
Are the days of Demaratos so full of vexation;
Many cares, much thinking and therefore

Not one moment of joy has Demaratos;
For this is not joy he is conscious of—
(It is not; he refuses to admit it;
How can he call it joy? His sorrow is crowned)—
When events show him clearly
The Greeks are going to come out victorious."

Demaratus was King of Sparta 510–491 B.C. Cleomenes by bribing the Delphic oracle and plotting with Leotychides obtained his deposition on the charge that he was illegitimate. Demaratus fled to the Persian court and accompanied Xerxes on his invasion of Greece. See Herodotus, bks. vi and vii.

101

SILVERSMITH

Upon this bowl of finest
Silver made.—
Which shall in Herakleides'
House be placed,
Where excellence and taste
Are chiefest laws—
Some dainty flowers, and thyme,
And many a cascade,
And in the midst a lovely
Naked boy,
I put in my design;
Him with one leg that played
Still in the water.—
Help me now, I prayed,
O memory of mine,
Now help me well to make
The boy I used to love,
His features to complete.
Much difficulty faced
My work because
Fifteen full years have gone
Over me since the day
He fell, a soldier, in the
Magnesian defeat.

The heading translated "Silversmith" means literally "An Artworker of Winebowls". The internal rhymes have been carefully preserved. For the defeat of Antiochus the Great by the Romans at Magnesia in 190 B.C., see no. 54. Malanos points out that the careful dating of the poem in the year 175 B.C. must be an intentional reference to a point in the early career of the notorious Herakleides, who soon afterwards went to Rome on an embassy on behalf of Antiochus Epiphanes, was banished by Demetrius Soter the successor of Antiochus in 162 B.C., and then supported the adventure of Alexander Balas. See nos. 54, 56, 80, 89, 97; and Polybius, XXVII, 17, and XXXIII, 14.

102

MELANCHOLY OF JASON SON OF KLEANDER

POET IN SYRIA KOMMAGÊNÊ, A.D. 595

The ageing of my body and appearance
Is a wounding from a horrible knife.
I have no long-suffering of any sort.
To you I have recourse, O Art of Poetry,
You in a way know something about drugs;
Attempts to numb the pain, in Imagination and Word.

It is a wounding from a frightful knife.—
Bring your drugs now, O Art of Poetry,
Which make the wound—for a time—not to be noticed.

103

FROM THE SCHOOL OF THE RENOWNED PHILOSOPHER

He remained a pupil of Ammonius Sakkas for two years;
But philosophy bored him and so did Sakkas.

Then he went into politics.
But he gave it up. The Governor was a fool;
And those around him official dummies with serious faces;
Their Greek, poor things, was super-barbarous.

His curiosity was rather attracted
By the Church; to be baptised
And pass for a Christian. But he soon
Changed his mind. It would certainly have meant a quarrel
With his parents, ostentatiously pagan;
And they would have cut off—frightful event—
At once their very generous contributions.

All the same he had to do something. He became a client
Of the corrupt houses of Alexandria,
Of every secret lair of debauchery.

Fate had been kind to him in this respect;
She gave him an extremely handsome appearance.
And he began to enjoy the divine endowment.

At least for ten years more
His beauty would last. After that—
Perhaps he might be going to Sakkas again.
And if meanwhile the old man were to die,
He would go to some other philosopher or sophist;
Somebody suitable is always to be found.

Or finally, to politics too it was possible
He might return—praiseworthily remembering
His family traditions, his duty to his country,
And other sounding matters of the sort.

Ammonius, called from his original occupation Sakkas, "corn-sack carrier", was a more or less Christian philosopher of Alexandria, who died A.D. 243, and is said to have been a teacher of Origen and Plotinus.

104

TO ANTIOCHUS EPIPHANÊS

The youth of Antioch
Said to the King,
"In my heart's core
Throbs a hope that is dear;
Macedonians once more,
Antiochus Epiphanes,
The Macedonians strain
In a struggle sore.
If only they could win—
I'd give to anyone
My lion and my ponies,
My Pan of coral, or
My Tyrian park and neat
Palace, and all, for all I own is
What you have given me,
Antiochus Epiphanes."

Some emotion stirred
The king perhaps.
But then he remembered
His father and his brother,
And he never spoke a word.
An eavesdropper might hear
Of something to repeat.—
And naturally another
Event brought on at Pydna
The unauspicious ending.

Antiochus Epiphanes was King of Syria 175–164 B.C. His father, Antiochus III the Great (223–187 B.C.), had been defeated by the Romans at Magnesia (see above, no. 54). His brother, Seleucus IV Philopator (187–175 B.C.), was assassinated. Seleucus Philopator's daughter Laodike married Perseus, last King of Macedon, defeated by Aemilius Paullus at Pydna 168 B.C.

105
THOSE WHO FOUGHT FOR THE ACHAEAN LEAGUE

Brave men were ye who fought and gloriously fell;
Of those, who had everywhere conquered, not afraid.
Blameless were ye, if Diaios and Kritolaos were at fault.
Whenever the Greeks shall be minded to boast,
"Our people turns out men like these," they will say
Of you. So wonderful shall be your praise.—

Written by an Achaean in Alexandria
The seventh year of Ptolemy Lathyros.

Kritolaos was a general of the Achaean League defeated by the Romans under Q. Caecilius Metellus Macedonicus in 146 B.C.; Diaios succeeded him in the command of the Achaeans, and was disastrously defeated near Corinth in the same year by L. Mummius Achaicus, and killed himself. Ptolemy VIII Lathyros (also called Philometor) was King of Egypt 117–107 B.C. and again 89–81 B.C.

106

IN AN OLD BOOK

In an old book—about a hundred years old—
Forgotten in between the pages
I found a watercolour without signature.
It must have been the work of a very capable artist,
It bore the title "A Representation of Love".

"—Of love for the extremely sensual", would be more
    appropriate.

Because it was evident when you looked at the work
(The idea of the artist was easily understood)
That for as many as love more or less wholesomely,
Within the bounds of what is at all permissible,
This boy was not intended
In the drawing—with his deep chestnut coloured eyes,
With the exquisite beauty of his face,
The beauty of unnatural attractions;
With those ideal lips which bring
Delight to a body that they love;
With those ideal limbs modelled for beds
Called shameless by current morality.

EPITAPH OF ANTIOCHOS KING OF KOMMAGÊNÊ

Returning from his funeral, in grief,
The sister of the temperate, the mild,
The much lettered Antiochos, the King
Of Kommagênê, on an epitaph decided.
And the Ephesian sophist Kallistratos—who resided
Often in Kommagênê's little state,
And, to the royal house often confided,
Had been a welcome visitor of late—
Wrote, on a plan the Syrian courtiers guided,
And sent this epitaph to the old lady.

"The glory of Antiochos, beneficent King,
Worthily, Kommagenians, let us sing.
Prudence was his, and justice for the weak;
He was wise and generous in his governing;
And then he was that best of all things, Greek—
No quality more precious has mankind :
What lies beyond only the gods may find."

Kommagênê was a district of northern Syria on the Euphrates, with its capital at Samosata, which was allowed to remain an independent kingdom after the Roman conquest of Syria in 64 B.C., and had several kings called Antiochus before it was finally incorporated in the Roman Empire in A.D. 72.

108

JULIAN SEEING NEGLIGENCE

"Seeing therefore that there is great negligence
Of the Gods among ye"—he says with grave aspect.
Negligence. But what then did he expect?
He might work at religious organisation,
As much as he liked, write to the Galatian High Priest,
Or other such, exhort him and direct.
His friends were not Christians; that was the situation,
But they could not even play,
As he could himself (a Christian born and bred)
With the setting-up of a new church, at least
As ridiculous in conception as in application.
After all they were Greeks. Nothing, Augustus, in excess.

Julian, called the Apostate, Roman Emperor A.D. 361–363, tried to reintroduce paganism as a religion of great austerity organised on a foundation of neo-Platonic philosophy. The opening quotation is taken from one of his letters addressed to Theodorus appointing him High-priest "of all the temples in Asia" (*Julian*, ed. W. C. Wright, Loeb Classics, Letter 20; vol. III, p. 56). Another letter (no. 22 in the same edition) is addressed to Arsacius, High-priest of Galatia. The last line of the poem may have been suggested by another letter (no. 21 in the same collection) which is a letter of remonstrance to the people of Alexandria on the murder of the Arian bishop George, the enemy of Athanasius; this letter ends with the remark that he administers only the mildest of remedies to them because he understands that they are of Greek origin and still bear traces of their ancient nobility and generosity.

109

THEATRE OF SIDON

A.D. 400

A worthy citizen's son—
                    And a good-looking boy
Of the theatre, better still—
                    Pleasing in more ways than one,
I now and then compose
                    In the Hellenic tongue
Extremely daring verses,
                    And these I circulate
Very secretly, of course—
                    O gods! They mustn't see them,
The people who walk about
                    All in dark clothes and talk about
Morality—my songs of joy;
                    Exquisite joy that comes when
The love of it is sterile
                    And rejected of men.

110

DESPERATION

He has completely lost him.
And now longs to discover
On lips that accost him
Of every new lover
Those lips of his; and when
He is in the embrace
Of any new lover,
Longs to be cheated over
Him, and think that he's the same,
And give himself to him.

He has completely lost him,
As if he'd never been.
He wanted—so he said—
He wanted to recover
From the lust that is branded,
And for sickness is a cover;
From the lust that is branded
And for shame is a cover.
There was still time—he said—
To fly and to recover.

He has completely lost him,
As if he'd never been.
Still in imagination,
By some hallucination,
On lips of other boys
He longs to discover
Those lips, and be a prover
Of his love once again.

III

JULIAN IN NICOMEDIA

Business that has no purpose and that seeks
Danger. And praise for ideas of the Greeks.

Enthusiasm for the old gods. Heathen shrines
That must be visited. Miracles and signs.

Chrysanthius and his frequent conversations.
Maximus—his philosophic lucubrations.

Naturally Gallus shows in these conditions
Uneasiness. Constantius has suspicions.

There is no doubt that his advisers are
Unwise. Mardonius says it has gone too far;

Means must be found at all costs to restrain
The rumour of it.—Julian goes again

To the Church of Nicomedia as a reader,
There in a loud voice, all devotion's leader,

He reads the Holy Writ. The audience
Throngs to admire his Christian reverence.

Julian the Apostate had to conceal his anti-Christian beliefs before he became Emperor (see no. 108). His brother Gallus was executed by the Emperor Constantius in A.D. 354. Maximus of Ephesus, a Neo-platonic philosopher, was one of Julian's teachers. Mardonius was his tutor, a scythian to whom he was handed over after his seventh year; see Julian's *Misopôgôn*, 352; (*Julian*, Loeb Classics, vol. II, p. 460).

112

BEFORE TIME SHOULD CHANGE THEM

Great was the grief
Of both at their parting.
It was not their will;
Only circumstances.
The needs of a living
Obliged one of them
To go far away—
New York or Canada.
Their loving of course
Was no longer the same;
It had started to chill
By degrees; the attraction,
Had started to chill,
The attraction and thrill.
But to be parted
Was never their will.
Only circumstances.—
Or perhaps like an artist
Fate made an appearance
Parting them now
Before feeling should fade,
Before Time should change them:
The one for the other
Will seem to stay ever
Twenty-four years old
The handsome boy still.

113

IN ALEXANDRIA, 31 B.C.

Coming from his little village, that lies just
Near the suburbs, still covered with the journey's dust,

The trader arrives. "Frankincense", and "Gum", his ware,
And "Best Olive Oil", and "Perfume for the Hair"

He cried along the streets. But in the noisy herd,
The music, the processions, how can he be heard?

The moving crowd around him jostles, hustles, thunders.
At last bewildered, What's the madness here? he wonders.

And someone tosses him too the gigantic piece
Of palace fiction—Antony's victory in Greece.

In 31 B.C. Antony, with Cleopatra, was disastrously defeated by Octavian at Actium, off the west coast of Greece; and he killed himself at Alexandria in the following year.

114

JOHN KANTAKUZEN PREVAILS

He sees the fields that still belong to him
With the corn, and the cattle, and the trees laden with fruit.
And farther away the house on the family estate,
Full of clothes, and precious furniture, and silver plate.

They'll take it from him—Jesus Christ!—All now to be their loot.

Would Kantakuzen have pity now if he found him
And fell at his feet? They say he was lenient,
Very lenient. But the army? And those around him?—
Or should he turn to the Lady Eirene, implore and lament?

Fool! To mix himself up with Anna's party—
As if it wasn't enough that Master Andronikos ever went
And married her! Have we ever seen a bent
Of competence in her, have we seen a core
Of humanity? Why even the Franks don't respect her any more.
Her plans were ridiculous, her preparations something to pity.
While they were threatening the world from within the City,
Kantakuzen had crushed them, crushed them all had Master Jack.

On the death of the Byzantine Emperor, Andronikos III Palaiologos in 1341, the new Emperor John V, his son, was only 11 years old, and although the Empire was threatened by external enemies there was a ferocious struggle for power between the dowager Empress, Anne of Savoy, and the Regent John Kantakuzen, who in 1347 was crowned joint Emperor as John VI. Eirene was his wife. The "Prelate" was the Patriarch John of Apri, described by Gibbon (ch. lxiii) as "a proud and feeble old man, encompassed by a numerous and hungry kindred". The description in the same chapter of the fortune and estates of Kantakuzen, taken from the description in Kantakuzen's own *Histories* (Bonn, vol. ii, p. 185, etc.), seems to have suggested the opening lines of the poem, which transfers this wealth to an unnamed magnate of the Empire who has involved himself in the civil war.

And to think he had meant to go over to Master Jack's
Side! And he would have gone. If he had, now fortune would
find him
Still a great prince, and with more strength behind him,
If only the Prelate at the last minute had not meant
To persuade him with his blandishment,
With his information wrong from beginning to end, his priestly
rulings,
His promises, and his tomfoolings.

115

HE CAME TO READ

He came to read. The books lie open,
Historians and poets, two or three.
He had hardly read for ten minutes when
He gave it up. Now on the sofa he
Is half asleep. He belongs entirely to books—
But he is very good-looking, and twenty-three years old;
Today in the afternoon love passed
Over his perfect flesh, and on his lips.
Over his flesh, which is the mould
Of beauty, passed love's fever, uncontrolled
By any ridiculous shame for the form of the enjoyment . . .

116

BY AN ITALIAN SHORE

Kêmos son of Menedoros,
A young Italiot,
Passes all his life
In elegant amusements;
In the manner which is
Theirs in Greater Greece
Where in wealth and riches
Young men are brought up.

Today he is sorely,
And against his nature,
Thoughtful and downcast.
Close by the seashore
He sadly sees before
His eyes they are unloading
Vessels with a store
Of Peloponnesian plunder.

Spoils of Grecian strife;
The plunder of Corinth.

Oh no today it's not,
Surely it is not right,
Not possible he might,
This young Italiot,
Feel for his amusements
Desire any more.

Italiot was the name given in antiquity to an inhabitant of Magna Graecia, "Greater Greece"; and Magna Graecia included southern Italy and Sicily, a district thickly planted with Greek colonies, many of which were well known for their wealth and luxury. Corinth was destroyed and sacked by the Romans in 146 B.C., when "the works of art which were not destroyed by the Roman soldiery were conveyed to Rome" (Smith's *Classical Dictionary*). (See above, no. 105.)

117

OF COLOURED GLASS

Much moves me one detail
At the crowning, in Blahernai, of John Kantakuzen
And of Eirene daughter of Andronikos Asan.
Seeing that they had only a few precious stones
(Great was the poverty of our distressful nation)
They wore artificial ones. A lot of bits of glass,
Red, green or blue. Nothing
That is mean or that is unseemly
Do they have in my eyes, those little bits
Of coloured glass. They seem on the contrary
Like a sorrowful protestation
Against the unjust misfortune of those being crowned.
They are the symbols of what it was fitting they should have,
Of what it was absolutely right they should have
At their crowning such a Lord John Kantakuzenos,
Such a Lady Eirene daughter of Andronikos Asan.

See above, no. 114. "Crowning" might refer either to a coronation or to a wedding ceremony. Actually there was a joint ceremony in 1347: the crowning of John Kantakuzen as joint emperor, and the wedding of his daughter Helena to John V Palaiologos. See Gibbon (ed. Bury), vol. vi, p. 503 (ch. lxiii)—a passage which seems to have inspired the poem—"Two emperors" [John V Palaiologos and John VI Kantakuzen], "and three empresses" [Anne of Savoy, Eirene Asan, and the thirteen-year-old Helena] "were seated on the Byzantine throne . . . The festival of the coronation and nuptials was celebrated with the appearance of concord and magnificence, and both were equally fallacious. During the late troubles, the treasures of the state, and even the palace, had been alienated or embezzled: the royal banquet was served in pewter or earthenware; and such was the proud poverty of the times that the absence of gold and jewels was supplied by the paltry artifices of glass and gilt leather." See also Finlay, *History of Greece*, vol. III, p. 446. Both passages are based on the description of the Byzantine historian Nicephorus Gregoras (Bonn, vol. II, pp. 788, 789).

118

TEMETHOS OF ANTIOCH

A.D. 400

Verses of young Temethos
The lovelorn poet. He's
Headed them just "*Emonides*"—
Of Antiochus Epiphanes
He was the dear companion;
Most beautiful indeed,
A youth from Samosata.
But if the verses were
Warm and affectionate
It is that "Emonides"
(From that ancient
Period: in the year
A hundred and thirty seven
Of the kingdom of the Greeks!—
Perhaps a little earlier)
Was put into the poem
As a bare name; and yet
A fitting name it is.
A love of Temethos
The poetry expresses

Malanos points out that the year A.D. 400 had a special significance for the poet, as marking the last days of Hellenistic paganism. (Cf. above, nos. 94 and 109.) Antiochus Epiphanes reigned in Syria 175–164 B.C. He is not known to have had a friend called Emonides; but he notoriously tried (in the words of the *Classical Dictionary*) "to root out the Jewish religion and to introduce the worship of the Greek divinities". The Syrians referred to the dynasty of the Seleucids as "the Kingdom of the Greeks". See the words of the Apocrypha, I Maccabees i. 10. "And there came out of them a wicked root, Antiochus surnamed Epiphanes, son of Antiochus the King, who had been an hostage at Rome, and he reigned in the hundred and thirty and seventh year of the Kingdom of the Greeks." Seleucus Nicator, the Macedonian founder of the Syrian monarchy, reigned 312–280 B.C., and the 137 years are counted from his accession.

Lovely and worthy of him.
We the initiate,
His own close friends and dear,
We the initiate
We know for whom
The verses were composed.
The men of Antioch read,
Unknowing, "Emonides".

119

APOLLONIUS OF TYANA IN RHODES

About proper education and conduct
Apollonius was speaking with a certain
Young man in Rhodes beginning to construct
A most luxurious house. "In a temple, I,"
Said the man of Tyana finally, "When I pass by,
Would much rather see therein, even if it be small,
A statue of ivory and gold
Than find in a large temple a cheap image of clay."

The "clay" image and "cheap"; the abominable after all.
And nevertheless some few (whom training has failed to
instruct)
It tricks them like a cheapjack. The base image of clay.

For Apollonius of Tyana, see also nos. 47, 91. The incident is taken from the *Life of Apollonius* by Philostratus (bk. V, ch. 22). The words quoted were used by the sage in rebuking a young man of Rhodes who admitted that he had already spent twelve talents, and proposed to spend as many more, on the building and decoration of his house, but had spent nothing on his own education.

120

IN THE DREARY VILLAGE

In the dreary village where he works—
An employee in a commercial firm,
Very young—and where he must alight
Waiting still for two or three months to pass,
Two or three months still for business to fall off,
So that he can move into town and throw himself
Into amusement at once and all the movement;
In the dreary village where he must alight—
He lay on his bed tonight sick with what love meant,
All his youth in desire of the flesh alight,
In a lovely tension all his lovely youth.
And in his sleep delight came to him; in his sleep
He sees and holds the form and flesh he wanted . . .

There are only two rhymes in this; and one of them is one of the poet's identical or homophonous rhymes (*anaménei*, *anaméné*) which has been reproduced in the two senses of "alight".

121

THE TWENTY-FIFTH YEAR OF HIS LIFE

He goes to the wineshop regularly
Where they had met last month.
He asked; but they knew nothing to tell him.
From their words, he understood he had got to know some
Person altogether unknown;
One of the many unknown and suspicious
Youthful forms that used to pass that way.
He goes however to the wineshop regularly, at night,
And sits and looks towards the entrance;
To the point of fatigue looks towards the entrance.
Perhaps he may walk in. This evening perhaps he'll come.

For nearly three weeks he does this.
His mind has grown sick with longing.
The kisses have remained on his mouth.
All his flesh suffers from the continuous desire.
The touch of that body is upon him.
He wants to be one with it again.

Not to give himself away, he tries of course.
Sometimes he hardly heeds.—
To what he is exposing himself knowing,
He has decided. Not improbably the life he leads
To scandalous disaster may be going.

122

THE ILLNESS OF KLEITOS

Kleitos, an attractive
Youth, about twenty-three years old—
Of excellent breeding, with a rare knowledge of Greek—
Is seriously ill. The fever found and seized
Him, which harvested this year in Alexandria.

The fever found him exhausted too and morally diseased
By grief that his companion, a young actor, had ceased
To love him, to want him, and no longer cares.

He is seriously ill, and his parents are frightened.

And an old servant who brought him up,
She is frightened too for the life of Kleitos.
And in her dreadful anxiety
There comes into her mind an idol
She used to worship as a little girl, before she came there as a
servant,
To the house of Christian notables, and turned Christian.
She takes secretly some sort of cakes, and wine, and honey; and
bears
Them before the idol. All she remembers of the airs
Of the litany she sings; odds and ends. The silly woman,
How little the black divinity cares
If a Christian gets well or not, she never grasps in the least.

In line 8, the words "no longer cares", not in the original, have been put in for the sake of the rhyme.

123

IN THE TAVERNS

Down in the taverns
And in the bordellos
Of Beirut I wallow.
I did not want to stay
In Alexandria, not I.
Tamides has left me;
He went with the son
Of the Prefect, and all for
A villa on the Nile,
A palace in the town.
I would not stay in
Alexandria, not I.
But in the taverns
And in the bordellos
Of Beirut I wallow.
In cheap debauchery
Somehow I exist.
The only thing that saves me
Like an enduring beauty,
Like a fragrance that over
My flesh has remained,
Is that for two years
I had Tamides for my own,
The most wonderful boy,
Mine, and not for a house
Or a villa on the Nile.

124

SOPHIST LEAVING SYRIA

You estimable don,
Now leaving Syria,
Who about Antioch
Intend to write a book,
In this your work, Mebes
Is worthy of your mention.
The very famous Mebes
Who's undeniably
The youth who is loveliest,
The one who is loved best
In the whole of Antioch.
None of the other boys
Of the same way of living,
Not one of them they pay
As dearly as for him.
In order to have Mebes
For two or three days only
They very often give him
Up to a hundred staters.—
I said, In Antioch;
But not in Alexandria,
And not even in Rome,
Can any boy be found
As charming as Mebes.

The gold *stater* is said to have been worth about twenty-five shillings. "Don", in this context, seems to be a suitable substitute for "sophist".

125

IN A TOWNSHIP OF ASIA MINOR

The news about the result of the seafight, at Actium,
Were certainly unexpected.
But there is no need for us to compose a new address.
Let only the name be changed. Instead of (there
In the last lines), "Having delivered the Romans
From the disastrous Octavius,
The burlesque Caesar,"
Now we will put, "Having delivered the Romans
From the disastrous Antony."
The whole text fits in beautifully.

"To the conqueror, to the most glorious,
In every warlike action unsurpassed,
Admirable in political achievement,
On whose behalf the township cordially did pray
The domination of Antonius."
Here, as we said, the alteration: "Of Caesar,
Regarding it as the fairest gift of Zeus—
To the mighty defender of the Greeks,
With his approval honouring Grecian manners,
In each and every Greek domain beloved,
Eminently indicated for illustrious praise,
And for the recording of his deeds at length
In the Greek language both in verse and prose,
The Greek language that is the messenger of fame,"
And all the rest of it, and all the rest of it. Everything
fits in splendidly.

At the battle of Actium in 31 B.C. Antonius was defeated by Octavius. See above no. 113. Mr. T. Malanos, in the work previously referred to, says that among his notes he has found a record of the following words of the poet himself about this poem: "It is a poem representing the changing mentalities of the (small) Greek towns, during the struggles for power of the Roman dictators, struggles which could have no beneficial effect on these towns—towns in fact for which it was completely indifferent whether the ruler of the world was called Antony or Octavius."

126

JULIAN AND THE CITIZENS OF ANTIOCH

> "The letter CHI, they say, had never done their city any harm, nor had the letter KAPPA. . . . And we having found some to explain . . . were given to understand that these were the initial letters of two names, and stood the one for Christ, and the other for Konstantios."
>
> Julian's *Misopôgôn*

Was it possible that they should ever deny
Their comely way of living; the variety
Of their daily recreations; their splendid
Theatre where they found a union of Art
With the erotic propensities of the flesh!

Immoral to a certain, probably to a considerable extent,
They were. But they had the satisfaction that their life
Was the much talked of life of Antioch,
The delightful life, in absolutely good taste.

Were they to deny all this, for to give their minds after
all to what?

To his airy chatter about the false gods,
To his annoying chatter about himself;

Cf. nos. 108, 111, and below, nos. 127, 154. The Emperor Julian's systematic attempts to disestablish Christianity and restore paganism were very badly received at Antioch which he visited in A.D. 362. Some of his difficulties are described in his own work *Misopôgôn* (*The Beard-hater*), addressed to the people of Antioch, which begins as a good-natured, if rather pedantic satire on his own bearded austerity, but soon degenerates into a puritanical scolding. The quotation in the heading is from the *Misopôgôn*, 357 A (*Julian*, Loeb Classics, vol. II, p. 474). Constantius was his cousin and predecessor on the Imperial throne.

To his childish fear of the theatre;
His graceless prudery; his ridiculous beard.

Most certainly they preferred the letter CHI,
Most certainly they preferred the KAPPA—a hundred
times.

127

A GREAT PROCESSION OF PRIESTS AND LAYMEN

Of priests and laymen a procession,
All the professions being represented,
Passes through the streets, the squares, and the gates
Of the renowned city of Antioch.
At the imposing great procession's head
A lovely, a white-vestured youth is holding
In upraised hands the Cross,
Our power and our hope, the holy Cross.
The gentiles, formerly so overweening,
Hurriedly now with diffidence and retrogression
Withdraw themselves from the procession.
Far from us, far let them remain for ever
(As long as they deny not their error). Onward goes
The holy Cross. Wherever in godly fashion
The Christians live, in every quarter,
It brings comfort and joy:
They come out, the devout, to the doors of their
houses
And full of exultation worship it—
The power, the salvation of the world, the Cross.—

It is a yearly Christian festival.
But today it is celebrated, you see, more openly.

Just after his visit to Antioch Julian was killed fighting against the Persians (A.D. 363), and Jovian was elected emperor by the army. Jovian was a Christian, though a tolerant one. He only reigned seven months. See above, no. 126.

One rhyme, linking lines 1, 10, 11, 14, has been reproduced. Another, linking lines 5, 13, 15, 20, has had to be omitted.

The procession with the "white-vestured youth" is suggested by a passage in Julian's *Misopôgôn*, 362 A (*Julian*, Loeb Classics, vol. II, p. 486).

The state has been redeemed at last.
The most unclean, the abominable
Julian reigns no more.

For the most pious Jovian let us pray.

128

PRIEST OF THE TEMPLE OF SERAPIS

That good old man my father,
Who loved me just the same always;
That good old man my father I am mourning
Who died the day before yesterday, a little before
daybreak.

Jesus Christ, that I may keep
The precepts thy most holy church adorning,
In every deed of mine, in every word,
In every thought, is my endeavour
Day after day. As many as deny thee
I do abominate.—But now I am mourning,
In lamentation, O Christ, for my father
Although he was—a dreadful thing to say—
At the accursed Serapion a priest.

The famous temple of Serapis at Alexandria, the Serapieion or Serapeum, was destroyed during the persecution of the pagans initiated by the Emperor Theodosius in A.D. 392.

129

ANNA DALASSÊNÊ

Alexios Comnenos a golden bull
Published to show the honour dutiful
He bore his mother, the very intelligent
Lady Anna Dalassêna—her deeds the token
Of worthy character;—from so much praise
And diverse, let us here convey one phrase,
A beautiful and noble sentiment,
"Never those cold words, mine or thine, were spoken."

Alexios I Comnenos was Emperor A.D. 1081–1118. This Golden Bull, appointing his mother Regent of the Empire, is quoted by his learned daughter Anna Comnena in her history of her father's reign (*Alexiad*, bk. III, ch. 6).

130

GREEK FROM OF OLD

Antioch boasts about
Its splendid monuments,
About its lovely streets;
About the surrounding
Countryside astounding,
And the great multitude
Of those who dwell therein.
It boasts it is the seat
Of many glorious kings;
About the artists too
And the wise men it has,
About the opulent
And the judicious merchants.
But more incomparably
Than all else Antioch
Boasts that it is a city
Greek from of old; so far goes
As kin of ancient Argos,
As that Ione, founded
By Argive colonists
To the honour abounding
Of Inachos his daughter.

The story that Io (the well-known heifer of the *Prometheus Vinctus* of Aeschylus), the daughter of Inachos, King of Argos, in her mad wanderings after her seduction by Zeus, came to Syria to die, and was traced by her brothers, who built a temple and a city, called Iopolis, in her honour, on the very site on which Seleucus Nicator the Macedonian afterwards founded the Syrian capital of Antioch; and that the citizens of Antioch continued to commemorate this ancient connection with Hellenic Argos—this story is told by the Byzantine sixth-century chronicler John Malalas, himself of Syrian origin (see *Malalae Chronographia*, Bonn, pp. 28–30). Mr. Malanos in the work to which I have so often referred, points out that Cavafy, next to Alexandria, had a special liking for Antioch, and would no doubt have been very pleased to discover that Antioch, like Alexandria, had some claim to call itself "Hellenic from of old". See above, no. 108.

131

DAYS OF 1901

It was this in him that was so distinctive,
That in the middle of all his dissoluteness,
And with his great experience of desire,
In spite of all the customary, in him,
Harmonisation of his age and attitude,
There were chance moments—but of course
They were very rare—when he gave
The impression of a flesh almost untouched.

The beauty of his nine and twenty years
Which had been so much put to pleasure's testing,
At moments it recalled surprisingly
A youth who—rather awkwardly—to love
Surrenders his pure body for the first time.

132

TWENTY-THREE TO TWENTY-FOUR

From half past ten he was in the café,
And was waiting for him soon to appear.
Midnight went—and he was still waiting for him.
It was gone half past one; it had emptied now
The café completely almost.
He got tired of reading newspapers
Mechanically. Of his three solitary shillings
Only one was left: such a long time he was waiting
He spent the others on coffees and on brandy.
He smoked all his cigarettes.
Such a long wait exhausted him. Because
Alone too as he was for hours, there began
To overtake him troublesome thoughts
Of his misguided life.

But when he saw his friend come in—at once
Tiredness, distress, consideration fled.

His friend brought him an unhoped-for piece of news.
He had won, at the gambling-house, sixty pounds.

Their good-looking faces, their wonderful youthful-
ness,
The sensuous love they had between them,
Were refreshed, livened, invigorated
By the sixty pounds from the gambling-house.

And all joy and strength, sensation and beauty,
They went—not to the houses of their respectable
families
(Where, besides, they were not wanted any more):
But to a house they knew, a very special one,

A house of ill fame; they went and asked for
A bedroom, and expensive drinks, and they went on
drinking.

And when they had finished the expensive drinks,
And when by this time it was nearly four o'clock.
They gave themselves happily to love.

133

DAYS OF 1896

He was disgraced completely.
An amorous inclination,
One stringently forbidden,
Looked down upon, and chidden
(Although it was inborn),
Was a sufficient cause;
The community was
Extremely puritan.
He lost by slow degrees
His money, not a lot;
Position after that,
And all his reputation.
Now he was nearing thirty
Without having made one
Year's livelihood by work,
At least that one could scan.
Sometimes he used to earn
His expenses where
To be a go-between
Is thought to be shameful.
He became such a sort
That with one of his station
If one often sees
You, you are compromised.

And yet not only this;
So much would not be fair.
Beyond this it is proper
To mention his beauty.
There is a point of view
Seen from which he appears
More attractively guised;
Appears a simple, genuine,

Child of love, who began,
Above his honour's ban,
Above his reputation,
To set not hesitating
The pure flesh that gives
Pure pleasure to man.

Above his reputation?
But the community
So very puritan
Had all its values wrong.

134

A YOUNG ARTIST IN WORDS IN HIS TWENTY-FOURTH YEAR

Work, brain, in any way you can now.—
He is being wasted by a halved enjoyment.
He is in an enervating situation.
He kisses the loved face every day,
His hands on the most wonderful limbs.
Never before has he loved with such a great
Passion. But the lovely realisation
Of love is wanting; wanting the realisation
Which both must long for with intensity.

(They are not both equally given to irregular pleasure.
Him only it has mastered absolutely.)

So he is wasting away and becoming completely neurotic.
Besides he has no work; that too contributes a lot.
Some small sums of money
He borrows with difficulty (almost
Goes begging for it sometimes) and pretends to keep himself.
He kisses the adored lips; and on
That wonderful body—but now he understands
That it only consents—he finds his pleasure.
And then he drinks and smokes; drinks and smokes;
And drags himself round the cafés all day long,
Painfully drags the pining of his good looks.—
Work, brain, in any way you can now.

135

IN A GREAT GREEK COLONY

200 B.C.

That things in the Colony are not going to perfection
Not the least doubt bears inspection,
And although somehow or other we do get along,
Perhaps it is time, as a good many think, to bring in a strong
Man to Reform the Constitution.

But the great difficulty and the objection
Is that they make a business erection
Of everything they talk about redressing,
These Reformers. (It would be a blessing
If nobody ever wanted them.) For the solution
Of the smallest detail they have questions and examinations,
And at once get into their heads the most radical alterations,
Insisting that they must be carried out without delay.

They also have a great liking for sacrifices.
"You must give up that profit, don't be sentimental:
Your enjoyment of it is precarious: in the Colonies today
It is just such increments which exact their prices.
This income of yours—some restitution;
Of this connection again some diminution;
And thirdly, something less: only the natural prosecution
Of a system; what else can you do? They seem fundamental;
But create a responsibility which is detrimental."

And as they go ahead with their inquisition,
They keep on finding superfluities, for abolition;
Things however that it is very hard for a man to put away.

And when, with luck, they have finished their work of direction,
And, after arranging and trimming everything little and long,
They depart, not without the proper collection

Of their salary, let us just see what the surgeons have left,
After so much expert execution.—

Perhaps it is not yet the moment, perhaps we were wrong.
We must not hurry; hurry is dangerous without circumspection.
Premature measures only bring repentance.
Undoubtedly and unfortunately the Colony has many irregu-
larities for correction.
Imperfect? Does anything human escape that sentence?
And after all, you see, we are getting along.

136

PICTURE OF A YOUTH TWENTY-THREE YEARS OLD

PAINTED BY HIS FRIEND OF THE SAME AGE, AN AMATEUR

He finished the picture
Yesterday at midday. Now
Looks at it in detail.
He has painted him in
A grey unbuttoned coat,
A dark grey; and without
A waistcoat or a tie;
And in a rosepink shirt;
And open at the throat,
So something may be seen
Of its beauty, a sight
Of breast and neck breathing.
His forehead on the right
All of it is nearly
Covered by his hair,
His beautiful and bright
Hair (as he thinks the right
Way to part it this year).
There is the expression
Completely sensuous
He wanted to put in
When he was doing the eyes,
When he was doing the lips . . .
His mouth, his lips which are
For the fulfilment of
Exquisite lovemaking.

137

UNDERSTOOD NOT

Concerning our religious opinions—
The silly Julian said: "I read, I understood,
I condemned." As if he had annihilated us,
He, most ridiculous, with that "condemned" of his.

Such cleverness though will not go down with us
Christians. "You read, but understood not; for if you had understood,
You would not have condemned", we answered at once.

The Emperor Julian the Apostate's criticism, of three words in the original Greek, will be found among the fragments of his Letters in the Loeb Classics edition, vol. III, p. 302. It is quoted in his *Ecclesiastical History* (5. 18) by the fifth-century writer Sozomen, who says it was addressed by Julian to the Bishops to show his contempt for their christianised versions of the ancient classics, or of the Homeric version of the Psalms composed by Apollinaris the learned Bishop of Laodicea. The answer of the Bishops, as quoted in the last lines of the poem, are also given by Sozomen.

138

KIMON SON OF LEARCHOS

TWENTY-TWO YEARS OLD STUDENT OF GREEK LITERATURE (IN KYRÊNÊ)

"The end came over me
When I was fortunate.
Hermoteles had me his
Inseparable friend.
My last days of all,
Although he was pretending
Not to be uneasy,
I noticed very often
His eyes were after weeping.
And when he thought a while
I had fallen asleep,
He would fall like a madman
On the end of my bed.
But we were both of us
Lads of the same age,
Twenty-three years old.
Fate is treacherous.
Perhaps some other
Passion would have taken
Hermoteles from me.
Fair was my ending; in
Our undivided love."—

This epitaph for Marylos
Aristodemos' son
Who died a month ago
In Alexandria,
I received in mourning,
I his cousin Kimon.
It was the writer sent it,
A poet whom I knew.

He sent it to me too
Because he knew that I
Was kin to Marylos;
And nothing else he knew.
My soul is full
Of grief for Marylos.
We had grown up together,
Like brothers, we two.

I am in deep melancholy.
His premature death
All resentment of mine
Has put out completely . . .
All resentment of mine
Against Marylos—though
He had stolen from me
The love of Hermoteles.
So if he wants me now,
Hermoteles, again,
It will not be the same.
I know my character
And sensibility.
The image of Marylos
Will be coming between
Us, and I shall think that
He is saying, "You see,
Now you are satisfied,
See, you have taken him back
As you wanted to, Kimon;
See, you have no excuse to
Be slandering me now."

139

IN SPARTA

King Cleomenes did not know, he did not dare—
He did not know how he could speak so plain
A sentence to his mother: that Ptolemy required
She should be sent to Egypt, and that he should retain
Her there in guarantee of their agreement;
A very humiliating and unseemly proposal.
And he kept on beginning to speak; and hesitating;
And he came to his opening words; and kept on stopping there.

But this excellent lady understood him
(She had besides heard some rumours about it),
And she began to encourage him to explain.
And she laughed; and she said that of course she was going.
That in fact she was glad she could be
In her old age of use to Sparta still.

As for the humiliation—but she did not care.
A descendant of Lagos, yesterday's child, could never under-
stand
The pride of Sparta; wherefore his demand
Could never in fact prepare
Humiliation for a Princess
Illustrious as she was, mother of a Spartan King.

Cleomenes was King of Sparta 236–222 B.C. Ptolemy III Euergetes, King of Egypt, promised to help him in his war against Macedonia and the Achaean League if he would send his mother Cratesicleia and his children to Egypt as hostages. This incident is taken from Plutarch (*Life of Agis and Cleomenes*, § 43; North's *Plutarch*, 1631, pp. 815, 816). See also below, no. 146.

140

DAYS OF 1909, 1910, AND 1911

Of a very poor and struggling seaman
(From an Aegean Island) he was the son.
Worked at an iron-smith's. His clothes shabby, the boots too
He had to work in pitiably torn.
His hands were dirty with rust and oil.

In the evening, when the shop closed, if he wanted to buy
Anything much, wanted perhaps to try
Some rather expensive tie,
Some tie for Sunday, or happened to spy
In a shopwindow some blue
Shirt of particularly lovely dye,
He would sell his body for a dollar or two.

I ask myself if of old great Alexandria knew
A youth whose loveliness with his could vie,
A boy more perfect than he was—now forgotten and lost:
Of course no statue or drawing of him was done; forlorn
Into a blacksmith's shop he was just tossed,
And soon by heavy labour there outworn
He was destroyed by suffering and cheap debauchery.

141

A PRINCE FROM WESTERN LIBYA

He was generally liked in Alexandria,
The ten days that he stayed there,
The prince from Western Libya
Aristomenes, son of Menelaos.
Like his name, his dress too was, tastefully, Greek.
He would accept honours gladly, but did not seek
Them; he was so unassuming.
He bought books, Greek
Books, of historical and philosophical critique.
And above all a man of few words.
He must be a deep thinker, people said,
And such men by their nature rarely speak.

He was neither a deep thinker, nor anything else.
Just an ordinary, ridiculous man.
He took a Greek name, he dressed like the Greeks,
He learned to behave like the Greeks more or less;
And he was afraid in his heart of accidentally
Spoiling a rather good impression
By frightful barbarisms in speaking Greek,
And then the Alexandrians would catch him on the raw,
As is their very unfortunate habit.

That was why he would confine himself to few words,
Attending fearfully to his cases and his weak
Pronunciation; and he suffered no little discomfort
Having whole conversations stacked inside him.

142

ON THE MARCH TO SINOPE

Mithridates, full of glory and power,
Of great cities lord and master,
Possessor of strong armies and fleets,
Going towards Sinope passed along a road
In the country very remote
Where a soothsayer had his dwelling.

Mithridates sent one of his officers
To ask the soothsayer how many good things
He should still acquire in the future, how many other powers.

He sent an officer of his, and then
Towards Sinope continued his march.

The soothsayer withdrew to a secret room.
After about half an hour he came out
In deep thought, and said to the officer,
"Satisfactorily I could not discern.
The day today is not suitable.
Some shadowy things I saw. I did not understand very well.—
But the King should be content, I think, with all that he has.

Plutarch in his *Life of Demetrius* (King of Macedonia 340–283 B.C.), wishing to show that Demetrius was "of a noble and courteous nature and that he dearly loved his friends", tells how he saved the life of Mithridates II, King of Pontus (387–302 B.C.), who was then a young man at the court of his father Antigonus. Antigonus, after a disquieting dream, which seemed to warn him that young Mithridates was dangerous, decided to put him to death. But Demetrius having been told by his father, under a vow of silence, about the proposed execution, as soon as he was alone with his young friend, "he wrote on the ground with the end of his dart, Mithridates looking on him: *Flie Mithridates*. Mithridates found straight what he meant, and fled the very same night into Cappadocia." (See Plutarch, *Life of Demetrius*, § 4; North's *Plutarch*, p. 886). A later Mithridates, Mithridates V Euergetes, King of Pontus, 156–120 B.C., is the hero of the present poem. He was assassinated at Sinope by conspirators of his own court; this incident of his meeting with the soothsayer appears to be invented.

Anything more will bring him into dangers.
Remember to tell him this, officer:
With all he has, in God's name, let him be content!
Fortune has sudden changes.
You must tell King Mithridates:
Very rarely is there to be found that noble companion
His ancestor had, who timely with his spear
Writes on the ground, to save, FLY MITHRIDATES."

143

MÝRÊS: ALEXANDRIA

A.D. 340

When I heard of the disaster, that Myres was dead,
I went to his house, although I avoid
Going into the houses of the Christians,
Especially when they have mournings or holidays.

I stood in a passage. I did not want
To go farther inside, because I noticed
That the relations of the dead boy were looking at me
With evident perplexity and with displeasure.

They had him in a large room
Of which from the end where I stood
I could see something; all valuable carpets,
And vessels of silver and gold.

I was standing and weeping at one end of the passage.
And I was thinking that our gatherings and our excursions
Would not be worth while any more without Myres;
And I was thinking I should not see him any more
At our lovely and disorderly nights-out,
Enjoying himself, and laughing, and reciting verses
With his perfect sense of Greek rhythm;
And I was thinking that I had lost for ever
His beauty, that I had lost for ever
The youth whom I adored passionately.

Some old women, near me, were speaking quietly about
The last day he was alive—
On his lips continually the name of Christ,
In his hands he was holding a cross.—
Afterwards there came into the room

Four Christian priests, and began to say prayers
Fervently and supplications to Jesus,
Or to Mary (I don't know their religion well).

We knew, of course, that Myres was a Christian.
From the first hour we knew it, when
The year before last he joined our gang.
But he lived absolutely like us.
More given to our pleasures than any of us;
Scattering his money unsparingly in our amusements.
About the world's esteem regardless,
He would throw himself gladly into rows at night

When our gang happened
To meet an opposing gang in the street.
He never spoke about his religion.
In fact once we told him
That we would take him with us to the Serapion.
But he seemed to dislike
That joke of ours; I remember now.
O and two other times come into my mind now.
When we were making libations to Poseidon,
He withdrew from our circle, and turned his looks away.
And when enthusiastically one of us
Said, "Let our company be under
The favour and protection of the great
The all-beautiful Apollo"—Myres whispered
(The others did not hear) "Excepting me".

The Christian priests in loud voices
Were praying for the young man's soul.—
I noticed with how much diligence,
With what strained attention
To the formalities of their religion, they were preparing
Everything for the Christian funeral.
And suddenly there mastered me a strange
Impression. Indefinitely, I felt

As if Myres was going from my side;
I felt that he was made one, a Christian,
With his own people; and that I was becoming
A stranger, quite a stranger; I noticed besides
A doubt coming over me: perhaps I had even been tricked
By my own passion, and had always been a stranger to him.—
I rushed out of their dreadful house,
I fled quickly before it should be seized, before it should be
changed
By their Christianity, my memory of Myres.

144

IN THE SAME SPACE

Environment, of house, of city centres, city quarters
Which I look upon and where I walk; years and years.

I have created you in the midst of joy and in the midst of sorrows;
With so many circumstances, with so many things.

And you have been made sensation, the whole of you, for me.

145

ALEXANDER JANNAIOS AND ALEXANDRA

Successful and completely satisfied,
The King Alexander Jannaios,
And his consort the Queen Alexandra
Pass with music before them in attendance
And with every sort of luxury and resplendence,
Pass along the streets of Jerusalem.
The work has succeeded brilliantly,
Which was begun by the great Judas Maccabaios
And his four illustrious brothers;
And afterwards was continued unremittingly in the midst
Of many dangers and many difficulties.
Now nothing remained that was unbecoming.
Ended was all subjection to the arrogant
Monarchs of Antioch. Behold
The King Alexander Jannaios
And his consort the Queen Alexandra
In all respects equal to the Seleucids.
Good Jews, pure Jews, faithful Jews—above all.
But, just as circumstances required,
Also conversant with the Greek speech;
And having relations with Greeks and with
Greek-mannered monarchs—but as equals, and no mistake.

Alexander Jannaios (Jonathan) reigned as King of the Jews at Jerusalem 104–77 B.C., son of Joannes Hyrcanos and brother of Aristobulus I whom he succeeded and whose widow Alexandra (Salome) he married. He obtained a hold on his kingdom by judicious massacres and confirmed it by numerous victorious expeditions against his neighbours. Malanos refers to Renan, who notes that the coins of Alexander and of Alexandra bear Greek as well as Hebrew inscriptions. Cf. I Maccabees xi. 74; xii. 1, 2. "So there were slain of the heathen that day about three thousand men: but Jonathan returned to Jerusalem. Now when Jonathan saw that the time served him, he chose certain men, and sent them to Rome, for to confirm and renew the friendship that they had with them. He sent letters also to the Lacedemonians, and to other places, for the same purpose."

Indeed it has succeeded brilliantly,
Succeeded manifestly
The work which was begun by the great Judas Maccabaios
And his four illustrious brothers.

146

COME, O KING OF THE LACEDAEMONIANS

Cratesicleia did not deign
The world should see her weeping and lamenting;
Majestical she proceeded and taciturn.
Nothing displayed her tranquil presence
Of her grief and of her tormenting.
But however be it one moment she let herself go;
And before she went on the unhappy ship to go to Alexandria,
She took her son into the temple of Poseidon,
And when they were alone she embraced him,
And kissed him, "perceiving that his heart yearned", says
Plutarch, "and he was convulsed for sorrow".
Yet her strong character strove;
And coming to herself the wonderful woman
Said to Cleomenes "Come, O King
Of the Lacedaemonians, when we go out
Of the temple, see that no one see us weeping
Or doing anything unworthy of Sparta.
For that alone is in our power; for the rest
Our fortunes, whatever god be giving, attend us."

So she went into the ship, going towards that "giving".

See above, no. 139; and the passage from Plutarch's *Life of Cleomenes*, and North's *Plutarch*, there referred to. The quotations from Plutarch in the poem are given in North's translation, but considerably adapted to make it more literal.

147

LOVELY FLOWERS AND WHITE

He entered the café
Where they used to go.—
Here it was his friend
Told him three months ago,
"We haven't got a farthing.
Two of the poorest boys
We are—and come down to
The places that are cheap.
I tell you plainly,
With you I cannot
Go about. Someone else
You must know, wants me."
This other one had promised
Him two suits and some
Silk handkerchiefs.—
To get him back again
He moved the earth, and
Somehow raised twenty pounds.
He went with him again
For the twenty pounds;
Yes and, besides that,
For their old friendship,
For their old love,
For their deepest feeling.—
The "other" was a liar,
A proper scoundrel;
Only one suit he had
Had made for him, and
Even that unwillingly,
With a thousand askings.

But now he does not want
The suits any more,
He doesn't want at all

The handkerchiefs of silk;
Neither twenty pounds
He wants, nor twenty pence.

They buried him on Sunday,
At ten in the morning.
They buried him on Sunday
A week ago nearly.

On his cheap coffin
He put some flowers for him,
Lovely flowers and white,
And they suited well
His beauty and
His two and twenty years.

At evening when he went—
He chanced to have business,
A need of breadwinning—
To the café where
They used to go together
A knife in his heart
Was the dark café where
They used to go together.

There are a few rhymes in the original which have been omitted in translation.

148

HE WAS ASKING ABOUT THE QUALITY

From the office where he had been given a place
Quite insignificant and poorly paid
(About eight pounds a month; perquisites included)
He came out when his lonely task concluded
Which all the afternoon had kept him bending:
He came out at seven o'clock, and slowly brooded
Loitering in the street.—Good looking;
And interesting; he seemed to have reached the spending
Of his full perceptual capacity.
He was turned twenty-nine a month ago.

He was loitering in the street, and in the poor
Alleys which led towards his own dwelling.

He was passing in front of a little shop
Where they sold different sorts
Of imitations and cheap things for workmen,
When he saw in there a figure, he saw a face
Which pulled him, and he went in, pretending
He wanted to see some coloured handkerchiefs.

He began to ask in a strangled voice
About the handkerchiefs, in a voice that seemed to fade
With lust, about the quality and the price.
And the answers came accordingly, absent-minded,
In a voice that was muted and made
Quite low, veiling an underlying consent.

They kept saying something about the purchase—and eluded
The only object, that their hands should touch
Over the handkerchiefs, that they should approach

Their faces and their lips as if by chance;
A bodily contact's momentary grace.

Quickly and secretly, so that the shopkeeper
Sitting at the far end should notice nothing.

149

THEY OUGHT TO HAVE THOUGHT

I have come down almost to homelessness and penury.
This fatal city, this Antioch
Has eaten up all my money:
This fatal city with its expensive life.

But I am young and in excellent health.
I have a wonderful mastery of Greek
(Aristotle, Plato, I know them forwards and backwards:
And orators, and poets, and anything you mention).
Of military matters I have a notion,
And I have friendships with leaders of the mercenaries.
I have plenty of entries to administrative things too.
In Alexandria I stayed six months last year;
I have some acquaintance (and that's useful too) with things there:
The views of the Grand Bad Man, and his tricks, and all the rest of it.

Wherefore I believe that I fill the bill,
Marked out to be of service to this country,
My own dear land of Syria.

Whatever work they put me to I will endeavour
To be of use to the country. That is my purpose.
If on the other hand they hinder me with their systems—
We know how clever they are: shall we talk straight?—
If they do hinder me, it isn't my fault.

I shall apply to Zabinas first,
And if that fool doesn't appreciate me,
I shall go to his opponent, to Grypos.
And if that idiot too won't take me on,
I go straight off to Hyrcanos.

One of the three at any rate will want me.

And my conscience is easy
As to the indifference of my choice.
All three of them do Syria the same amount of harm.

But I'm a ruined man, it isn't my fault.
I have misfortunes and I'm trying to mend them.
The almighty gods ought to have seen about
Creating a fourth man and an honest one.
I should have been delighted to work with him.

"Grand Bad Man" is an attempt to reproduce the Greek *Kakergetes* ("malefactor"), a nickname of Ptolemy *Euergetes II*, ("benefactor") commonly known as Ptolemy *Physcon* ("bladder") King of Egypt 146–117 B.C.

Alexander called *Zabinas* was a pretender who, with the backing of Physcon, seized the throne of Syria in 128 B.C. He defeated Demetrios II Nicator, but was afterwards (122 B.C.) defeated and killed by Antiochus called *Grypos* ("hooknose") who himself reigned at Antioch 125–96 B.C.

Hyrcanos, son of Simon Maccabaeus, founder of the Judaean monarchy which culminated in Herod, reigned 135–106 B.C.

150

THE MIRROR IN THE HALL

The rich house had in the hall
An enormous mirror, very old;
Bought at least eighty years ago.

A very handsome boy, assistant at a tailor's
(On Sundays an amateur athlete),
Was standing there with a parcel. He handed it
To someone of the house, and he took it inside
To fetch the receipt. The tailor's assistant
Was left alone, and waited.
He went up to the mirror and began to look at himself
And put his tie straight. After five minutes
They brought him the receipt. He took it and went away.

But the old mirror which had seen, and seen,
In the many years it had been
In existence, thousands of things and faces;
The old mirror was glad now
And was proud to have received upon itself
That entire beauty for a few minutes.

151

ACCORDING TO THE MAGIC PRESCRIPTIONS

"What distillation can be found from herbs
Of enchantment," said a certain sensualist,
"What distillation according to the prescriptions
Of ancient Grecosyrian sorcerers made
Which for a single day (if for no more
Its power suffices), or even for a little while
My three and twenty years should bring me back
Again; my friend at two and twenty years
Should bring me back again—his beauty, his love.

"What distillation can be found by the prescriptions
Of ancient Grecosyrian sorcerers made
Which, in accordance with that turning-back,
Our little room should also bring again?"

152

IN THE YEAR 200 B.C.

"Alexander the son of Philip and the Grecians excepting the
Lacedaemonians"—

We are able very well to imagine
How completely unaffected they must have been at Sparta
By that inscription: "Excepting the Lacedaemonians".—
But naturally. They were not, the Spartans,
To be led about, and to be ordered about
Like valuable servants. And besides
A panhellenic expedition without
A Spartan king for leader
Would not have appeared to them of much standing.
O most certainly "excepting the Lacedaemonians".

That too is an attitude. It can be understood.

And so, "excepting the Lacedaemonians" at the Granikos;
And afterwards at Issos; and at the final
Battle, where was swept away the fearful host
Which the Persians had concentrated at Arbela,
Which moved off from Arbela for victory, and was swept away.

And out of that wonderful panhellenic expedition,
The victorious, the illustrious,
The renowned, the glorified
As none has been glorified else,
The incomparable expedition: we have come out
A new Greek world and great.

We: the Alexandrians, the men of Antioch,
The Seleucians, and the numerous
Greeks over above of Aegypt and of Syria,
And those in Media, and those in Persia, and all the others.

With our far-reaching dominations,
With various influence prudently adapted.
And our Greek Common Speech
Into the midst of Bactria we carried it, even to the Indians.

Talk about the Lacedaemonians now!

The three great battles in which Alexander the Great overthrew the Persians were fought at the River Granicus (334 B.C.); at Issus (333 B.C.); and near Arbela (331 B.C.).

See Plutarch's *Life of Alexander the Great*, § 16 (and Arrian, I, 16, 7); North's *Plutarch*, p. 681: "And because he would make the Grecians partakers of this victorie, he sent unto the Athenians three hundred of their targets, which he had won at the battell; and generally upon all the other spoiles he put this honourable inscription: Alexander the sonne of Philip, and the Grecians, excepting the Lacedaemonians, have wonne this spoile upon the barbarous Asians."

In the first line of the poem this inscription is quoted. An unnamed Greek (probably one of those Greeks from Alexandria with whom the poet likes to identify himself) is supposed to be reading this inscription in 200 B.C. (a hundred and thirty years after Alexander's victories) and to be meditating on the Hellenisation of Asia which had resulted from Alexander's expedition; an expedition in which the Lacedaemonians from Sparta had been too proud to take part. The causes and circumstances of their abstention are obscure, but it is known that they alone of the Greek states refused to send delegates to the congress at Corinth in 338 B.C. which elected Philip of Macedon, Alexander's father, head of the Greek confederacy.

153

DAYS OF 1908

That was the year when he stayed
Without work; for his living played
Cards, or backgammon; or borrowed and never paid.

He was offered a place at a small
Stationer's, three pounds a month. It didn't suit him.
It was not decent pay at all.
He refused it without hesitation;
He was twenty-five, and of some education.

Two or three shillings a day he made, more or less.
From cards and backgammon what could a boy skim,
At the common places, the cafés of his grade,
Although he played sharply, and picked stupid players.
As for borrowing, that didn't always come off.
He seldom struck a dollar, oftener he'd fall
To half, and sometimes as low as a shilling.

Sometimes, when he got away from the grim
Night-sitting, for a week at a time or more,
He would cool himself at the baths, with a morning swim.

The shabbiness of his clothes was tragical.
He always wore the same suit, always displayed
A suit of cinnamon brown discoloured and frayed.

O summer days of nineteen hundred and eight, I recall
The picture of you, and out of it seems to fade,
Harmoniously, that cinnamon suit discoloured and frayed.

The picture of you has preserved him
Just as he would take off, would fling down
The unworthy clothes, the mended underclothes,

And remain all naked; faultlessly beautiful; a wonder.
Uncombed and lifted up his hair was;
His limbs a little sunburnt
From the morning nakedness at the baths and on the beach.

The elaborate rhyme pattern in the first part has been preserved exactly by the addition of the words "never paid" and "frayed" which are not explicit in the original.

154

ON THE OUTSKIRTS OF ANTIOCH

We were amazed at Antioch when we heard about
The latest goings-on of Julian.

Apollo had it out with this gentleman, at Daphne!
He wouldn't give an oracle (we were worried!),
He had no intention of speaking prophetically, unless
His precinct at Daphne was purified.
The neighbouring dead, he declared, were disturbing him.

At Daphne there were many graves.
One of those there entombed
Was the wonderful, the glory of our church,
The holy, the triumphant martyr Babylas.

The false god was hinting at him, was afraid of him.
As long as he felt him near he didn't dare
To bring out his oracles: not a word.
(The false gods are terrified of our martyrs.)

The unholy Julian tucked up his sleeves,
He was nervy and began to shout: "Take him up, remove him,
Take this Babylas away at once.
D'you hear? Apollo is disturbed.
Take him up, get hold of him at once.
Exhume him, take him wherever you like.
Take him away, turn him out. Is this a joke?
Apollo said his precinct should be cleaned."

We took it up and carried it to another place, the holy relic;
In honour and in love we took it up and carried it away.

And that did the precinct a fine lot of good.
There was no delay at all, and a fire,

A great fire started, a terrible fire;
And the precinct was burned up, and Apollo too.

The image was a cinder; to be swept away, with the rubbish.

Julian was ready to burst and he gave it out—
What else could he have done?—that the fire was put there
By us Christians. Let him go on talking.
It has not been proved; let him go on talking.
The fact is he was ready to burst.

The Christians of Antioch had buried the body of their bishop Babylas in the grove of Apollo at Daphne on the outskirts of the city; Julian had the body removed; and that same night (October 22, A.D. 362) the temple of Apollo, which Julian had restored, was destroyed by fire. See Julian's *Misopôgôn*, 361 B ff. (Julian's works in the Loeb Classics, ed. Wilmer Cave Wright, vol. II, p. 484, with editor's note ad loc.). See above, nos. 108, 126, 127.